TUIAVII'S
WAY

TUIAVII'S WAY

A SOUTH SEA CHIEF'S COMMENTS ON WESTERN SOCIETY

by Chief Tuiavii and Erich Scheurmann

Adapted and translated into English by Peter C. Cavelti

Legacy Editions

Legacy Editions Ltd.

Toronto, Ontario - Canada

The speeches of Chief Tuiavii were first published in 1920 under the title
"Der Papalagi—Die Reden des Südseehäuptlings Tuiavii aus Tiavea,"
by Felsen-Verlag, Buchenbach, Baden, Germany.

The manuscript was translated into English by Peter C. Cavelti, who also
wrote the special introduction and epilogue contained in this volume.

The design of this book and its cover were conceived by Richard Moore;
the cover photograph is reproduced from an original by Thomas
Andrew, entitled "Tattooed Samoan," ca. 1893. Background photography:
Russell L. de Kord.

Legacy Editions Ltd.
Suite 220
3219 Yonge Street
Toronto, Ontario M4N 2L3
Canada

ISBN 0-9682469-0-7
Manufactured in the United States of America

"The term 'Savage' is, I conceive, often misapplied, and indeed when I consider the vices, cruelties and enormities of every kind that spring up in the tainted atmosphere of a feverish civilization, I am inclined to think that so far as the relative wickedness of the parties is concerned, four or five Marquesan Islanders sent to the United States might be quite as useful as an equal number of Americans dispatched to the Islands in a similar capacity."

Herman Melville, *Typee*, 1846

CONTENTS

INTRODUCTION

I was first told about Chief Tuiavii's[1] manuscript in 1971 by a fellow back-packer I met in Mexico and who has ever since been my friend. When he got back to Switzerland and I to Canada, he mailed me a copy, which I read in one sitting. I liked it so much that I vowed on the spot I would translate it into English some day. Shortly after, I lost the book.

More than twenty years later, in 1992, I decided to re-focus on my project. In the meantime, the steadily growing need for greater balance in our hectic, competitive and often unrewarding lives had become apparent to a much larger segment of our society. The unconditional surrender to anything technological, scientific and economically satisfying which had dominated the past century seemed to have come to at least a halt, if not an end. The limits of economic growth were one reason, but the deep desire to lead a more spiritual life loomed equally large. The publishing industry,

[1] Tuiavii is pronounced *Too-ee avee*.

among others, had capitalized on this new awareness, yet among all the learned essays, new book titles and lectures to which I had access, nothing came close to the sensation I had felt when I first read Tuiavii's story. Was it that I had been younger and more idealistic, or was there more to it?

I was sufficiently intrigued to start a global search for a copy of Tuiavii's work, which I knew had been published in Germany in 1920 under the title *"The Papalagi—the speeches of the South Sea Chief Tuiavii of Tiavea."* I soon learned that a reprint had been published in 1977, but my mind was set on finding a copy of the original edition. After snooping around second-hand bookstores in New York, Toronto, London and Zurich and subscribing to several trade publications, I finally had the idea of writing to the roughly 300 book dealers who might be carrying titles of interest to anthropologists or historians. Surprisingly, I received more than a hundred letters back. All responses were negative, but some contained names of people who might be able to help me hunt down a copy. Among them were museum curators, anthropologists and university librarians, most of them in Holland and Germany. After doing as advised, I finally struck gold— two notices arrived almost simultaneously, but, surprisingly, from book dealers in New York and California. Miraculously, both had found a copy of the original 1920 printing of *Papalagi*! Within a few weeks, they were in my possession and I went to work.

The first thing I noticed when I re-read *Papalagi*, was that the years had not taken away any of its appeal. On the contrary, many of the South Sea Chief Tuiavii's impressions about his visit to Europe seemed even more relevant to me and the world I lived in, than they had more than two decades earlier. Thanks to our society's newly acquired appetite for spirituality,

INTRODUCTION

I now also had a better chance to gain an understanding of how Tuiavii's daily life in Samoa might have looked. I had become aware of the writings of Joseph Campbell, who splendidly articulates the things which "primitive societies" had and which are in our modernized world so sorely missed. Documentary films, like Lorne and Lawrence Blair's *Ring of Fire* and David Maybury-Lewis' *Millenium,* had shown me in a most dramatic way how myths, rituals and a tightly knit community could enrich our spiritually empty lives. And, finally, I had a far better understanding of colonial history, which helped me see Tuiavii's life and times in better perspective.

I believe this is the first time Tuiavii's manuscripts are published in English. Like all translators and editors, I was faced with the dilemma of whether I should "improve" on the author's words or leave them much as they were. Most of my changes were made where I

believed that literal translation (from the already translated German version) would distort the intended
emphasis. On some occasions, I also rearranged sen-
tence compositions and punctuation. I did so, because
certain modes of expression of turn-of-the-century
German can be irritating and confusing to today's
English reader. However, my overall rule was to stay as
true to the manuscript as possible.

Tuiavii expresses his thoughts in simple and childlike
language, which sometimes makes it appear repetitive
or even unimaginative. Especially in an age where attention spans are short and people have to make their
points fast or be ignored, Tuiavii is at a disadvantage.
The reader should remember that the author was a
Samoan who chronicled his impressions in a language
which did not have words for many of the things he
saw. We must also be patient with the sequence in
which Tuiavii took his notes. He did not mean for his

manuscripts, which were really intended as individual speeches, to be published. If he had known that they would be contained in one cohesive volume and arranged in chapters, he might have altered their sequence. The first speech, for example, which deals with the Western way of clothing, represents to us one of the less interesting aspects of our lives and may be less relevant today than other topics, with which the author deals later. But imagine how fascinating it must have been to South Sea islanders to hear about the large number of "skins" worn by Europeans, how these were arranged and on what occasions they were worn!

Some of Tuiavii's speeches resemble passages from the Communist Manifesto, but only if seen in the most narrow context. After all, these are the impressions of a Samoan who never had to put up with regular work and was suddenly caught in the swirl of the industrial revolution. When the author bemoans the white man's obsession with work and its standard of measurement, money, we should remember that Tuiavii was a child of distant islands, where it was possible to survive and, arguably, lead a comfortable life, without much toil.

Chapter after chapter, whether he touches on how our towns are constructed, how we use machines, our preoccupation with material things or our lack of time, Tuiavii always does a masterful job of describing our ways. Because he had never seen, or even imagined, many of the things which awaited him in Europe, his approach is to use so much detail that any Samoan could follow his description. The result is a commentary that is often like that of a child in awe. As a result, some readers will be tempted to dismiss Tuiavii's commentary as the simple-minded musings of yet another victimized colonial. Such an assessment would not only be unfair, but also incorrect. What makes this book different is precisely that its author does not fit that mold. Tuiavii is different in several ways, and I will explain why.

The most widely published writings and speeches dealing with the white man's advance into colonial territories are those of North America's Indian Chiefs. Invariably, they present us with the sad tale of how the newly found land was robbed of its resources, its wildlife decimated, its culture brutally suppressed and, finally, how any native standing up to such wanton terror was murdered without hesitation. Sweeping indictments like the well-known speech of Chief Seattle are "reports from the front" first hand accounts of how vile, deceptive and short-sighted the ways of the white man really were.

This makes them very effective, but deprives us of the moral odyssey to which Tuiavii subjects us. Chief

Seattle's words touch us deeply, but what he has to report is the wholesale destruction of his environment, his culture and his people—as a result, sadly, there is no moral dilemma. There is no doubt, from a historical or ethical perspective, that the white man committed a heinous crime and that its consequences are irreversible.

Now to Tuiavii, who lives in the Samoa of the late 1800s. The white man arrives and, to him, he is the "bringer of light," who introduces him to the teachings of Christ. We don't know exactly how old Tuiavii is at this time, but it is a good guess that he is a young man, if not an adolescent. Samoa, and the South Seas in general, had been an important discovery when they were mapped a century earlier by Captain Cook, but a colonial priority they were not. The white people who came here arrived with a different mission than those who colonized India, the Middle East or the Americas, all of which were plundered of their resources. The colonial agenda in Samoa was considerably more leisurely and less defined; maybe because it was annexed relatively late, maybe because there was a lot less competition between the major powers for a myriad of tiny islands which would be expensive and difficult to administer.

This spared Tuiavii and his "brothers of the many islands" from the cruel fate experienced by native populations elsewhere. The missionaries were the only colonial presence with zeal here, and they taught the natives to stop warring against each other. Whether for political reasons or motivated by Christian doctrine, they told the islanders to hand over their "fire sticks," which they had earlier acquired as trade goods. In this way, they taught them the way of love and peaceful coexistence. To the idealistic Tuiavii this must have appealed immensely, as good and moral things always appeal to young people.

In 19th-century Europe it became common for specimens of various native populations to be toured in traveling shows, sometimes against their will. Captain Fitzroy of *Beagle*[2] fame, for instance, kidnapped five locals from *Tierra del Fuego*, after the theft of one of his whale boats. Later, the story goes, he nobly released his hostages, but not all wanted to go back, causing Fitzroy to take the Fuegians back to England. The three who survived the journey were renamed "Fuegia Basket," "Jemmy Button," and "York Minster" and given into the care of a clergyman. After studying English and Christianity, they were presented to the King and Queen. Tuiavii, also, came to Europe as part of a traveling show of natives from around the world, but he did not need to be kidnaped or even enticed.

---

2   The ship on which Charles Darwin traveled to the Galapagos Islands

So impressed was he with the ways of the white man—the *Papalagi*—that his sole passion became to visit Europe. In short, Tuiavii's experience is incomparably different from that of natives in other parts of the world, in that to him colonization seemed a positive force, so much so that he wished to go and emulate the ways of the "bringers of light." As a consequence, Tuiavii's insights into the white man's life are gained in Europe. Hence, this is not a report from the front, as are the speeches and writings left to us by the great Indian chiefs, but a journal which started as a travelogue and ended up becoming a report written "behind enemy lines." Because in Europe, the author's idealistic notions are gradually shattered. He realizes that the way of love and sharing, as preached by the missionaries, is not a formula for success or even subsistence in Europe. To him, the way of life in Victorian times resembles a path of darkness—haste, selfishness and greed are the predominant tools of survival;

hypocrisy is the theme of the times. He becomes aware that his own people, the South Sea islanders, had lived a life much closer to Christian doctrine than the Europeans, who had sent missionaries to Samoa! In time, he deeply resents this duplicity, but not before giving the *Papalagi* the benefit of the doubt.

Now Tuiavii's genius as a communicator reveals itself. Once he recognizes that the white man should be pitied and that his ways can never bring happiness to his people, he addresses the most important challenge of his life—how can he get his brothers to see the truth and stop them from being drawn into the white man's orbit? He does it by preparing a series of speeches—perhaps because public speaking is the traditional way to reach people; perhaps because it's the most immediate and controllable way to influence large audiences. In any event, Tuiavii's topics are carefully chosen and his presentation of each is ingenious.

Unfailingly, he centers on a theme that is of great fascination to his people, which is certain to draw them deep into the subject. Imagine a turn-of-the-century crowd of Samoan islanders being told about the white man's machines, or his professional life, or a movie! Tuiavii does this with such aplomb that he is sure to have endeared himself to his people as one of the great story tellers of his time. But his words also cast a spell over today's reader. The things he talks about are so common to us, that to hear them described in the minutest detail and in a vocabulary which, by necessity, makes heavy use of similes and images, is miraculous and enchanting.

Lastly, Tuiavii starts dealing with the moral dilemma. In the language of a child, he portrays what the white man could be doing with this or that invention or custom of his, and what he actually ends up doing. His discourse is invariably logical and objective, and during this part of the narrative, Tuiavii avoids making judgments. Because his mind is so innocent, we are drawn to the spectator stands, looking down at a grotesque play, which we recognize as the life of the white man. Now it is up to us to pass judgment. Only at the very end of each speech, when both his intended audience of islanders and today's readers have long made up their minds, does Tuiavii sum up his views. And now he leaves no doubt as to where he stands on the subject and how his people should act!

Tuiavii's speeches should have made him not only popular as a skillful storyteller, but also earned him a spot in Samoan culture as a great prophet, because his was indeed the way of the prophet. By observing and articulating the lessons of the present, he hoped to equip his people for the future. When he counseled them to leave the Europeans to their own vision of happiness, but to resist their effort to bring the white man's version of truth to his islands, he sought to prevent what seemed to him a nightmare. Tuiavii's legacy to today's Western reader is that he makes us see things from his perspective and, by doing so, leaves us with a deep sadness. That he does so without cursing our civilization, but instead merely describes us as victims of our own inventions is to his enduring credit and makes this a great book.

Tuiavii's speeches were brought to us by a German writer and adventurer, Erich Scheurmann, who was, and still is, a subject of great controversy. A good part of my epilogue is devoted to him. Scheurmann traveled to the Samoan islands and lived there for several years, at a time when only few others had visited the area. To his credit, he seems to have accepted Tuiavii's views without the prejudice which characterized his time.

Scheurmann's choice of title for Chief Tuiavii's speeches, *The Papalagi*, is intriguing. The word *Papalagi*, in Samoan, means "White Man," or "Master." Linguists tell us that the correct pronunciation is *pa-pa-lan-ghee*; they also comment that the literal translation of *Papalagi* is "he who breaks through the sky." Apparently, the first white missionary landing in Samoa arrived in a sailboat. The natives looked on from afar and mistook the gigantic sail for a hole in the sky, through which the white man had come to visit them.

Erich Scheurmann's rationale for printing the Tuiavii manuscript is less romantic, but not without idealism. He drily records the reasons for making available *Papalagi* "to the readers of Europe, without the author's permission and surely against his will." It's all based on his conviction that it could be of value "to us educated whites how our culture is viewed by one still tightly tied to nature. Through his eyes we will see for ourselves, from his perspective, what we can never again attain ourselves." Scheurmann speculates that "civilization fanatics" will dismiss Tuiavii's thoughts as naive, perhaps even ridiculous, but hopes that "the more reasonable and humble reader will soon be provoked in his thoughts and forced to see himself from the outside in, for [Tuiavii's] wisdom comes from simplicity, which is from God and does not originate in education." Scheurmann sees the speeches as nothing less than an appeal to all the "primitive tribes of the South Sea to pull away from the enlightened peoples of the European continent."

"When I first met Tuiavii," says Erich Scheurmann, "he lived peacefully and unaware of Europe's world" on the distant islet Upolu, which is part of Samoa. There, he was the master and highest chief of the village of *Tiavea*. Scheurmann's first impression was that of a friendly giant—about six feet tall and of unusually strong build. In contrast, his voice was "soft and mild as that of a woman." His large, dark and deep-set eyes were arched by a thick set of brows and his gaze was severe and rigid. Yet when addressed, Tuiavii's face would light up and betray his good-natured personality. Apart from this, nothing distinguished our subject from his native friends. He drank his *kava*[3], went to *loto*[4] each morning and evening, ate bananas, taro and yams and observed all native customs. Only those closest to him knew "how incessantly his spirit fermented and his mind searched for answers, even when he lay on his mat, his eyes closed as if dreaming."

"In general," muses Scheurmann, "natives, like children, live only in the realm of the senses and entirely in the present," without any regard for those outside their own small world. In this respect, we are told, Tuiavii was an exception. "He towered over his peers, be-

---

[3] Samoa's national drink, prepared from the roots of the Kava-plant
[4] Church service organized by the missionaries

cause he had that awareness, that inner strength, which divides us from primitive peoples." Scheurmann thinks it may have been that quality which gave rise to Tuiavii's desire to experience far-away Europe, a longing which had already existed when he visited the mission school, but which was to be fulfilled only in his adult years. Craving for knowledge, he eventually joined a traveling show which criss-crossed Europe. Later, he traveled through most of the continent, gathering information about each country's customs and culture. Scheurmann was frequently astonished how exact these observations were, and how Tuiavii recorded details others might have missed. He saw a thing for what it was and never, in all his observations, did he or could he leave his platform of objectivity.

Before presenting Tuiavii's notes, Scheurmann reminds us of another key point. "He views all of Europe's cultural achievements as a mistake, a dead end—he, the uncultured islander! This could appear arrogant, if not all were recounted with the wonderful innocence of a humble heart." There are other contradictions in Tuiavii, but Scheurmann's respect and admiration for him is apparent throughout. "He warns his fellow-natives, even implores them, to free themselves from the sway of the white man, yet he does it with the voice of regret and thus proves that his zeal originates in love and not in hatred." Only once does Erich Scheurmann actually quote his Samoan friend, presumably because what Tuiavii said touched him as deeply then, as it touches us today. Before the two friends parted for the last time, Tuiavii had this to say: "Your people thought they were bringing us light. But in reality you want to draw us into your darkness." By the time Scheurmann departed from Polynesia, carrying with him Tuiavii's manuscript written in his native language, he had serious questions about the world to which he was about to return.

INTRODUCTION

Scheurmann's adventures in Samoa and Tuiavii's quest to understand the white man make as good a story as life will write, but they harbor other, less obvious messages. Perhaps most vital among these is the recognition that we, the "civilized" ones, are attracted to the "raw" and "uncorrupted," because it transcends intellect and allows us to plunge into depths we cannot find in our excessively organized and rational world.

In Daniel Defoe's *Robinson Crusoe*[5], it is the cannibal "Friday" who profoundly influences the shipwrecked civilized Englishman. Here is how Crusoe sums up the attempt to teach Friday about his religious beliefs: "...in laying things open to him, I really informed and instructed myself in many things that either I did not know or had not fully considered before, but which occurred naturally to my mind upon my searching into them for the information of this poor savage. And I

---

5   *The Life and Strange Surprizing Adventures of Robinson Crusoe* was published in two parts in 1719 and 1720.

had more affection in my inquiry after things upon this occasion than ever I felt before; so that whether this poor wild wretch was the better for me or no, I had great reason to be thankful that ever he came to me."

Another South Sea novelist, Herman Melville, cast Queequeg into the role of the savage when he wrote *Moby Dick*[6]. Queequeg is the opposite of Ishmael, a civilized Christian, who is forced to share his quarters with him and is at first frightened by his alien appearance, his strangely tattooed skin and his pagan religious ritual. But later, Ishmael surprises himself as he recognizes that *his* belief system is profoundly changed by Queequeg, much as Robinson Crusoe found himself changed by Friday and Erich Scheurmann by Tuiavii. "I was a good Christian; born and bred in the bosom of the infallible Presbyterian Church. How then could I unite with this idolator in worshipping his piece of wood? But what is worship? thought I. Do you suppose now, Ishmael, that

[6] *Moby Dick*, or, *The Whale*, was published in 1851.

the magnanimous God of heaven and earth—pagans
and all included—can possibly be jealous of an insignifi-
cant bit of black wood? Impossible! But what is worship?—to do the will of God—*that* is worship. And
what is the will of God?—to do to my fellow man what I
would have my fellow man do to me—*that* is the will of
God. Now, Queequeg is my fellow man. And what do I
wish that this Queequeg would do to me? Why, unite
with me in my particular Presbyterian form of worship.
Consequently, I must then unite with him in his; ergo, I
must turn idolator. So I kindled the shavings; helped
prop up the innocent little idol; offered him burnt
bisquit with Queequeg; salaamed before him twice or
thrice; kissed his nose; and that done, we undressed and
went to bed, at peace with our own consciousness and
all the world."

Neither is this where the parallels end. Melville describes Queequeg much as Erich Scheurmann depicts

Tuiavii, with a "certain lofty bearing" . . . "like a man who had never cringed and never had a creditor." Like Tuiavii, Queequeg was also desperate to visit civilization. After being found hiding aboard a visiting whaling ship, he refused to leave, "throwing himself at full length upon the deck. . . . In vain the captain threatened to throw him overboard; suspended a cutlass over his naked wrists; Queequeg was the son of a king, and Queequeg budged not." Why this determination to experience the civilized world? It appears that the craving of the native to make contact with the white man, and thus realize his own potential, is as pressing as our desire to have our own belief system uprooted.

When reflecting on Tuiavii's and Scheurmann's respective voyage into each others' worlds, it is tempting to see the former through rose-colored glasses and underestimate the qualities of the latter. But we must

remember how difficult it must have been for
Scheurmann, the product of Europe at the beginning
of this century, to allow Tuiavii into his belief-system,
and to actually end up seeing many things from a
Samoan perspective. At the very least, it gives us an
appreciation of the man's tolerance.

When viewed in this context, it is particularly distress-
ing that Scheurmann in the end betrays Tuiavii. While
the islander returns from his hero's journey as a
prophet, bearing a message of great value to his people, the white man breaks his promise not to take this
message back to civilization. But then this is much the
way things were during Tuiavii's and Scheurmann's
time, when a colonialist agenda clashed with and forever altered much of the undeveloped world.

Peter C. Cavelti

ACKNOWLEDGMENTS

I would like to thank Thomas Mastronardi, who first told me about Chief Tuiavii's speeches. My friend Stephanie Rayner urged me to pursue my goal of translating the book into English and gave me new insights into Herman Melville's and Robert Louis Stevenson's South Sea literature, which greatly enriched my perspective on the subject matter. I deeply appreciate her support.

I am also very grateful to Jonathan Rabinowitz, who gave of his time and advice most generously and made it possible for me to gain access to Erich Scheurmann's other writings. Richard Moore helped extensively in designing this book; I am much indebted to him. My appreciation and gratitude also go to the many others, who contributed their energy and time, supported my work with enthusiasm and encouragement, and opened my mind to new perspectives.

ACKNOWLEDGMENTS

And, finally, I want to thank my best friend and wife, Carol, who assisted me with this project in countless ways and who helps me maintain what Tuiavii spoke of often and what is most precious in my life— my balance.

P. C. C.

THE SPEECHES

OF THE

SOUTH SEA CHIEF

TUIAVII

OF TIAVEA

HOW THE PAPALAGI COVERS HIS FLESH WITH MANY CLOTHS AND MATS

The *Papalagi* constantly tries to cover his flesh. "The body and its limbs are flesh; only what is above the neck is the true human," I was told by a white man who was well respected and counted as clever. He thought the only thing worthy of contemplation was the home of the senses and the place where both good and evil thoughts reside. Hence, the white man happily leaves his head and, if must be, his hands, uncovered. Even though head and hands are nothing but bones and flesh. Incidentally, he who leaves any other flesh uncovered, has no right to be viewed as properly behaved.

At the time a young man is married to a maiden he has no way of knowing whether he is being deceived, for he has never before seen her body. Even later she will show it to him rarely and when she does, only at night or in the twilight. A maiden, even one grown as beautiful as the fair *Taopou*[1] of Samoa,

Please note the following convention on footnotes in this section of the book: Literal translations from Samoan are not marked; explanatory footnotes from Erich Scheurmann's original edition are marked with the affix [ES]; explanatory footnotes by Peter C. Cavelti are marked [PCC].

covers her body, so that no one can see it or take pleasure in beholding her.

Flesh is sin, thus says the *Papalagi*. For he believes his mind is great after all his thinking. The arm which is being lifted in the sunlight to throw an object is an arrow of sin. The chest, which crests like a wave when it takes in air, is a vessel of sin. The limbs used by the maiden to give us the *Siva*[2], are sinful. And even the parts which touch to make humans so that the great earth is pleased, are sin. Everything is sin that is flesh. There is poison in every tendon, a treacherous venom which carries from human to human. Even he who merely looks at flesh soaks up the poison, is wounded, and is as evil and degenerate as the one who shows it. Thus are decreed the holy laws of the flesh of the white man.

[1] A legendary beauty
[2] A native dance

This is why the body of the male *Papalagi* is covered from head to toe with cloths, mats and skins. So thick and so tight are they that no human eye, no ray of sunshine can penetrate them. So thick are they that his body becomes as pale, white and tired as the flowers which grow in the deep forest. Let me tell you, understanding brothers of the many islands, what a burden each *Papalagi* carries on his body. At the very bottom, the body is wrapped by a thin white skin, which is gained from the fibers of a plant. The "upper skin" is thrown high, so that it can fall over head, chest, arms and down to the thighs. The "lower skin" is pulled from the bottom up, over the legs and thighs, up to the navel. Both skins are covered again through a third, thicker skin. This skin is woven from the hair of a four-footed woolly animal, which is bred especially for this purpose. This is the actual cloth and it consists of three parts, one covering the upper body, one the middle and the third protecting the thighs and legs. All three are held together by shells and strings made from the juices of the rubber tree[3], so that they appear as one. This cloth is usually grey like the lagoon during rainy season. Colors are not allowed, except that men who like to be noticed and run after women sometimes like the middle part to be colorful.

Finally, the feet are clad in a soft and then a very tough skin. The soft skin can be stretched and made comfortable, but not the tough one. It is made from the hide of a strong animal. Until it is totally hardened, the hide is held underwater, scraped with knives, beaten and put in the sun. Out of this hide, the *Papalagi* then builds high-rimmed canoes, just large enough to receive a foot; one for the left foot and one for the right foot. These vessels are then firmly tied to each foot with strings and hooks, so that the feet are then contained in a house, like the

---

3   Tuiavii describes buttons and rubber bands. [ES]

body of a sea-snail. These foot skins are worn by the *Papalagi* from dawn till dusk; he takes them on *malaga*[4], he dances in them and he wears them even when it's as hot as after a rain in the forest.

Because this is very unnatural, as the white man must know, and because the feet stink as if they were dead, and because most European feet can actually not grasp things or climb up a tree—because of these things, the *Papalagi* attempts to hide his clumsiness in the following way. He covers the red hide which makes up his foot skin with mud and then makes it so shiny by rubbing it that the eyes can no longer take it and have to look elsewhere. Once a *Papalagi* living in Europe became famous and many people came to see him, because he told them: "It isn't good that you carry such tight and heavy skins on your feet—walk barefoot under the sky when the dew of the night covers the grass and all sickness will flee from you." This man was very healthy and clever, but people ridiculed him and soon he was forgotten.

The white woman, too, carries many mats and cloths around her body and thighs, just as the men do. That is why her skin is covered with scars and sores from strings. The breasts are flat and can't yield milk from the pressure of the mat, which covers her from neck to lower body, both on her front and back. This mat is made from fishbones, wires and threads and is very hard. Because of this, many mothers have to give milk to their children in a glass roll, which is closed at the bottom and has an artificial nipple at the top. Nor is it their own milk that they give, but that of ugly, red, horned animals, from which it is taken by force from four tubes in their underbelly.

Incidentally, the cloths worn by women and maidens are thinner than those of men; they can also be colorful and are allowed to be beheld from afar. Also, neck and arms can often be seen through the cloth, so that more flesh is visible. Yet it is considered good when a maiden covers herself well; people then say with satisfaction: "She is chaste," which means that she observes the proper behavior. I never understood why at large *fonos*[5] and meals women and maidens are allowed to show their necks and backs, without this being thought of as a disgrace. But perhaps the spice of these special occasions is that things are allowed, which are normally forbidden.

Only the men keep their necks and backs fully covered at all times. From his neck down to his nipples, the *alii*[6] wears a shield stiffened with chalk, the size of a taro leaf. On it rests a high, white cloth ring,

[5] Social gatherings, meetings
[6] Master

also stiffened. Through this ring he pulls a colorful cloth, knots it like a boat line, then pushes a golden nail or a glass pearl through it and, finally, lets the whole thing hang over the shield. Many *Papalagi* also wear cloth rings around their wrists, but never at their ankles. The white shield and the cloth rings are very meaningful. A *Papalagi* man can never be seen without these, wherever there are women. Even worse than being without them is if the cloth rings are soiled and no longer carry light. That's why many high-ranking *aliis* change their breast shield and their cloth rings every day.

While the woman has many colorful cloths and mats for festive occasions—entire upright standing boxes full—and while she gives much thought to which cloth she might wear today or tomorrow or whether it should be long or short, and while she always talks lovingly of which ornaments she should hang from the cloths, the man usually owns only one festive cloth and rarely talks about it. This is the so-called bird-clothing, a deep black cloth, which ends in a sharp point on the back, like the wing of the bush parrot. With this cloth the hands must be covered with white skins; the skins are stretched over each finger, so tightly that the blood burns and runs to the heart. That's why it's acceptable that reasonable men carry these skins in their hands or tuck them into a skin worn around the body below the nipples.

As soon as a man or woman leave the hut, they cover themselves in yet another skin, which, depending on whether the sun shines or not, is thicker or thinner. They also cover their head, the men with a stiff, black vessel, bulging and hollow like the roof of a Samoa house; the women with large pieces of woven straw or baskets turned upside down, to which they attach flowers which never wilt, feathers, pieces of their cloths, glass pearls or other adornments. This makes them resemble the *tuiga*[7] of the *taopou* at the war dance, only that the *tuiga* is far more beautiful and cannot fall off the head, even in a storm or when dancing. The men constantly wave their head house to greet others, while the women delicately bend their weighty headgear forward, as if it were an unevenly loaded boat.

Only at night, when the *Papalagi* seeks the sleeping mat, does he throw all his cloths and skins aside, but then immediately cloaks himself in a new skin, which is open at the feet and leaves these uncovered. The nightskin of maidens and women is often richly adorned at the neck, although this cannot often be seen. As soon as the *Papalagi* lies down on his sleeping mat, he immediately covers himself with the belly feathers of a large bird, which are held

7 Ceremonial headgear

together in a huge cloth, so that they cannot separate and fly away. These feathers cause the body to sweat and make the *Papalagi* think he is lying in the sun, even when it doesn't shine. Because he does not like the real sun very much.

It should now be clear through all this that the *Papalagi's* body turns white and is without the color of joy. But this is how the white man likes it. The women, even more the maidens, are much concerned to protect their skin, so that the light never turns it red; that's why they hold a large roof over themselves, as soon as they step into the sun. As if the pale hue of the moon were more precious than the color of the sun. But the *Papalagi* loves to fashion wisdom after his beliefs and to craft a law to suit his wisdom. Because his nose is pointed like the tooth of a shark, it is declared beautiful, while ours, forever round and

without resistance, is thought ugly, even though
we believe the opposite.

Because the bodies of women and maidens are covered so abundantly, the men and youngsters have a
great longing to see their flesh, as is natural. They
think of this day and night and often describe the
body shapes of the women and maidens—always as
if what is beautiful and natural were sinful and
should happen only in the darkest shadows. If they
saw the flesh of a maiden when they met her, they
would give more thought to other things, their eyes
would not wander and their mouths would not
speak deceitful words.

But flesh is sin and is of the *aitu*[8]. Can you imagine
more foolish thinking, my brothers? If one could believe the words of the white man, one would wish
with him that human flesh should be as hard as the

---

8   The evil spirit, the devil

lava stone and without its beautiful warmth, which comes from the inside. But we should rejoice that our flesh can talk to the sun, that we can swing our leg like the wild horse, because no cloth hinders it and no foot skin ties it down, nor does anything fall off our head. Let us enjoy the sight of the maiden, who is graceful and shows her limbs in sunshine and moonlight. Foolish, blind and without a sense of joy is the white man, who has to cover himself so abundantly to be without shame.

OF THE STONE BOXES, STONE GAPS, STONE ISLANDS AND WHAT IS BETWEEN THEM

As in a seashell, the *Papalagi* lives in a firm encasement. He lives between stones as does the *skolopender*[9] between the cracks in lava. Stones are all around him, next to him and even above him. His hut resembles an upright box made of stone—a box with many compartments that is full of holes. Only in one spot is it possible to slip into the stone hut or come out of it. The *Papalagi* calls this spot "entrance," but only when he goes in. When he comes out, he calls it "exit," even though both are one and the same. At this spot there is a large wing made of wood, which must be firmly pushed in; only in this way can one get into the hut.

Most huts are inhabited by more people than can be found in a single Samoa-village, which is why one has to know exactly the name of the *aiga*[10] one wishes to visit. Because every *aiga* has a specific part of the stone box for itself, either on top, or

---

9   A type of centipede
10 Family

below, or in the middle; sometimes left or right, or up front. And often one *aiga* knows nothing of the other, absolutely nothing, as if not only a stone wall, but *Manono, Apolima* and *Savaii*[11] and many seas were between them. Often they hardly know each others' names and when they meet at the place where they slip in, they greet each other only with a reluctant nod or mumble to each other like hostile insects. As though they were offended that they have to live so close together.

If the *aiga* lives on top, under the roof of the hut, one has to climb many branches, sometimes zig-zag and sometimes round as in a circle, until one reaches the point where the name of the *aiga* is written on the wall. Now, one sees a delicate imitation of a nipple, which has to be pushed until it screams, which alerts the *aiga*. Next, someone looks through a small, round, hole in the wall which is covered

11 Three Samoan islands

with wire, to see if it is not an enemy who has come. Once a friend is recognized, the *Papalagi* unties a large wooden wing, which is firmly attached by chains, and pulls it inside, so that the visitor can slip through into the real hut.

This hut is again divided many times by stone walls, so that one slips through other wings, from one box to another, each becoming smaller. Each of these boxes, which are called by the *Papalagi* "rooms," has a hole. Larger boxes have two or three holes, through which light can enter. These holes are covered up with glass, which can be removed when fresh air is needed in the box, which is very necessary. Yet there are many boxes without a light- and air-hole. It wouldn't be long before a Samoan would suffocate in such a box, because there is no breeze, as in every Samoan hut. There are also the odors of the cookhouse, which cannot escape. But the air

which can be let in from the outside is not much
better and it's difficult to believe that people can live
here, that they don't turn into birds and grow wings,
in order to soar and fly where the air and the sun
are. But the *Papalagi* loves his stone boxes and
doesn't notice that they are not good for him.

Each stone box has its own purpose. The largest
and brightest is for the *fonos*[12] of the family or to receive visitors; another to sleep in. Here, the sleeping mats are kept, which means they lie freely on a
wooden platform with long legs, so that the air can
flow under the mats. A third box is to eat in and
make smoke clouds; a fourth to keep food stored, a
fifth to cook in and a last box, the smallest, is to
bathe in. This is the most beautiful box. It is covered by large mirrors, the floor is adorned with a
layer of colorful stones and in the middle stands a
large bowl made of metal or stone, into which run

12 Gatherings, meetings

both sun water and cold water. One can climb into this bowl, which is as large as the grave of a chief, to wash off all the sand from the stone boxes. There are huts with more boxes, too. There are even huts in which each child, each servant, and even the dogs and horses of the *Papalagi*, have their own box.

Between these boxes the *Papalagi* spends his life. Now he is in this box, now in that, depending on the time of day and hour. Here, his children grow up, high above the earth, often higher than the top of a palm—between stones. From time to time the *Papalagi* leaves his private box, as he calls it, to go into another box which is there for his work. There, he wishes to be undisturbed and cannot have his woman and his children around. During this time, the maidens and women are in the cookhouse, where they cook or shine foot skins or wash cloths

or mats. If the *Papalagi* is rich, then this work is
done by servants and the women go to visit others
or fetch food.

In this fashion, more people live in Europe than we
have palms in Samoa. Some may have a great longing for the forest and the sun and the light, but this
is generally viewed as an illness which must be
fought. If someone is not content with this stone life,
then others will say that he is an unnatural human
being, which is supposed to mean that he doesn't
know what God has intended for man.

These stone boxes stand in great multitude close to
each other, no tree and no shrub separates them,
they stand like people shoulder to shoulder, and in
each box there are as many people as in a whole
Samoa village. A stone's throw away, on the other
side, is an identical row of stone boxes, again

shoulder to shoulder and in these boxes again there live people. Between the two rows is only a small gap; the *Papalagi* calls this "street." This gap is often as long as a river and is covered with hard stones. One has to walk long to find an open space, but only to find that this is where other gaps come together. These again are as long as rivers and at their end, openings turn into stone gaps of equal length. In this way, one can get lost for days between the stone gaps, until one finally reaches a forest or finds a large piece of blue sky. Between the gaps one rarely sees the real color of the sky, because each box contains at least one, and sometimes several, fire places. The air is almost always full of smoke and ash, as it is near the great crater in *Savaii*. This ash rains into the gaps, so that the high stone boxes look like the mud in a mangrove swamp, and people end up with black soil in their eyes and hair, and hard sand between their teeth.

But this doesn't keep the people from walking around between these gaps from morning until night. Many even have a particular desire to do so. Especially in some gaps there is such a crowd that the people flow together like a dense syrup. These are the gaps where large glass cases are built into the boxes—all the things are laid out here, which are needed by the *Papalagi* to live: cloths and mats, headgear, hand and foot skins, food, meat and even real things to eat like fruit and vegetables, as well as many other things. They are spread out to lure people here. Yet no one is allowed to take anything, even if he really needs it. He first has to get an authorization and must make a sacrifice.

In the stone gaps there is much danger from all sides, because people are not just walking. There are others who ride and drive and are carried in large glass boxes, which glide on metal bands. The noise is great. Your ears are deaf, because the horses beat their feet against the stones on the ground and people bang their hard foot skins down. Children shout, men shout, with joy or out of despair—everyone shouts. You cannot be understood by anyone without shouting. There is a general humming, rattling, stamping and crashing as if you stood near the surf at *Savaii* on a day when the most terrible storm rages. Yet the crashing of the surf is cherished and doesn't rob you of your senses like the storm between the stone gaps.

Now all of this together: the stone boxes with the large number of people, the high stone gaps which flow everywhere like a thousand rivers, the people between them, the noise and rage, the black sand and smoke over everything, without a tree, without the blue of the sky, without clear air and clouds—all of this makes up what the *Papalagi* calls a "town."

This is his creation, of which is he very proud, even though here live human beings who have never beheld a tree or a forest, have never seen an open sky, and have never encountered the Great Spirit face to face. Humans who live like crawling insects in the lagoon, who make their home under the corals, although even the coral is cleansed by the fresh water of the sea and touched by the warm breath of the sun. Is the *Papalagi* really proud of the stones, which he has carried together? I don't know. The *Papalagi* is a being with particular feelings. He does much which doesn't make sense and makes him ill, but he praises it and sings himself a nice tune about it.

The town is what I have talked about. But there are many towns, small ones and large ones. The largest are those where the chiefs of the land live. The towns lie there spread out like islands in the sea. Sometimes they are only a swim away; often a day's journey. All stone islands are joined through marked paths. You can also drive on a land ship, which looks thin and long like a worm, constantly pushes out smoke and glides along iron strings at great speed, faster than a twelve-seater canoe[13]. Yet if you want to call as much as a *talofa*[14] to your friend on another stone island, you don't even need to walk or glide to him—you blow your words into metal threads, which stretch like long vines from one stone island to another[15]. Faster than a bird do your words get to the place which you have chosen.

Between all these stone islands is the actual land, which is called Europe. A part of this land is as fair and fertile as ours. There are trees, rivers and forests and there are real villages, as well. Even those huts which are made of stone are surrounded by fruit-bearing trees, so that the rain can wash them on all sides and the wind can dry them again.

13 By the late 1800s, passenger trains were in use around the world. [PCC]
14 A greeting; literally translated "I love you"
15 The telephone was invented in 1876 and the first telephone exchanges were installed in the U.S. and England within three years. [PCC]

In these villages live people with different feelings than those in the towns. They are called "country people." They have rougher hands and their cloths and mats are less clean than those of the gap people, even though they have more to eat.

Their life is much healthier and more beautiful than the life of the gap people. But they don't believe it and because the people in the town don't have to do much and don't have to reach into the earth to place its fruit in it and later harvest it, they envy them. They live in hostility with them, because they have to give food from their land to them, have to pluck the fruits which are eaten by the gap people, have to raise animals until they are fat and then hand over half. It is clear that they have to work hard to grow enough food for all the gap people and they can't understand why it is that the gap people wear more beautiful cloths than they do, have white hands and don't have to sweat in the sun or be cold in the rain.

This is not of much concern to the gap people. They are convinced that they have higher rights than the people in the country and that their labors have greater worth than placing fruit in the earth and taking it back. But the fight between these two parties is not such that there is war. In general, the *Papalagi* is content with things as they are, whether he lives between the gaps or in the country. The country people admire the realm of the gap people when they visit there, and the gap people sing high notes when they come to the country. The gap people leave the country people to raising their pigs, while the country people let the gap people build and love their stone boxes.

But we, who are free children of sun and light, want to be true to the Great Spirit and not burden our hearts with stones. Only lost, ailing beings, who no longer touch God's hand, can live happily between stone gaps without sun, light and wind. Let us leave the *Papalagi* with his dubious happiness, but let us destroy any attempt to place stone boxes on our sun-filled shores and to kill the joy of life with stone, gaps, dirt, noise, smoke and ash, as is his goal.

Of the Round Metal and the Heavy Paper

Sensible brothers, heed my words and be happy that you don't know the misery and terror of the white man. You can all attest that the missionary says "God is love." He says that a real Christian would do well to always hold in front of him the image of love. He says that this is why the white man should reserve his devotion to God alone. But he has lied to us and betrayed us; he was bribed by the *Papalagi* to trick us with the words of the Great Spirit. Because the round metal and the heavy paper, which is what they call "money," that is the true god of the white man.

Talk to a European of the God of love: he will think and then a smile comes over his face—he is smiling about the simplicity of your thought. But hand him a blank round piece of metal or a large heavy paper and immediately his eyes will light up and his lips will moisten. Money is his love, money is his God. All white people think of it, even when they sleep. There are many, whose hands have become crooked and whose posture has been bent like the legs of the forest ant, from grasping for metal and paper. There are many whose eyes have turned blind from counting money. There are many who have sacrificed their friends for money, their laughter, their honor, their conscience, their happiness, their woman and their children. Almost everyone loses their health to it, to the round metal and the heavy paper. They carry it in their cloths between hardened skins which are folded. At night they place it below their sleeping mats, so that no one can take it away from them. They think of it daily, hourly, every moment. All of them, all of them! Even the children! They have to think of it, must think of it. This is what their mother teaches them and what they observe from their father. All Europeans!

When you walk between the stone gaps of *Siamanis*[16], every few moments you hear a shout: "mark!" And again the same shout: "mark!" You hear it everywhere. In *Francia*—"franc"; in *Peletania*—"shilling"; in *Italia*—"lire." Mark, franc, shilling, lire—it's all the same[17]. All of these words mean money, money, money. Money alone is the true God of the *Papalagi,* just as it is the Great Spirit whom we worship the most.

However, it is not possible in these countries of the white man to be without money only once, from sunrise to sunset. Without any money you could not satisfy your hunger or still your thirst, nor could you find a sleeping mat at night. You would be put into the *fale pui pui*[18] and denounced in the *many papers*[19], because you were found without money. You have to pay—that means give money—for the ground on which you walk, for the soil on which stands your hut, for

16 Germany
17 France, England, Italy
18 Jail
19 Newspaper

spending the night on a sleeping mat, for the light which brightens your hut. You pay so that you can shoot a pigeon or bathe in the river. If you want to go where people are joyous, where they sing or dance, or if you want to ask advice from your brother, you have to give much round metal or heavy paper. You have to pay for everything. Everywhere is your brother who holds his hand open and despises you or curses you if you don't fill it. Your humble smile and friendly look doesn't help to soften his heart. He will open his mouth wide and scream at you: "Miserable one! Vagabond! Lazy lout!" This all means the same and is the greatest humiliation which can befall you. Even for your birth you must pay and when you die, your *aiga* has to pay: both for your death and for giving your body back to the earth, as well as for a great stone, which is placed on your grave in your memory.

Everyone will attest that I have found only one thing, for which no money is charged in Europe: breathing air. But I believe this is only so because it's been overlooked—if one could hear my words in Europe, round metal and heavy paper would immediately be charged for this as well. For all Europeans constantly look for new reasons to charge money.

Without money you are in Europe like a man without a head, a man without limbs. You need money, just as you need to eat, drink and sleep. The more money you have, the better your life. When you have money, you can get tobacco, rings or beautiful cloth for it. You can have as much tobacco, as many rings or as many cloths as you can pay for. If you have much money, you can have much. Everyone wants to have many things, which is why everyone wants to have much money. And each person wants more than the next. That's why there is greed and why the money is so vigilantly watched at every hour. Cast a round metal into the sand and the children will throw themselves on it, fight over it, and he who can capture and hold it is the victor and is happy. But money is rarely thrown in the sand.

Where does money come from? How do you get much money? Oh, in many ways, some easy and some difficult. If you cut off your brother's hair, if you take away the refuse in front of his hut, if you steer a canoe across the water or when you have a good thought. But, to be fair this must be said: even if every thing requires round metal and heavy paper, you can also easily get these. You need to do a thing which the Europeans call "work." "Work and you have money" is a rule of behavior in Europe.

Yet there is a great injustice with all this, about which the *Papalagi* doesn't think and doesn't want to think, because then he would have to admit to this injustice. Not everyone who has a lot of money also works a lot. Actually, everyone wants to have a lot of money without working much. This is how this comes about: when a white man earns so much money that he has food, a hut and a sleeping mat and beyond that a bit more, he immediately uses the money he has to spare to make his brother work. For himself! He gives him the work which before made his own hands dirty and hard. He lets him carry away the dirt, which he made. If it's a woman, she takes herself a girl as her worker. She lets her clean the soiled mat, the cooking pans and the foot skins and she makes her heal the torn cloths, but will not let her do anything which does not serve herself.

Now the *Papalagi* has more time for greater, more important and joyful work, which leaves the hands clean and the muscles relaxed—and for which more money is paid. If he is a boat builder, then the other now has to help him build boats. From the money which the helper should get for building boats he takes the greater part, and as soon as he can, he lets two brothers work for him, then three—constantly more people have to build boats for him, eventually a hundred or more. Until he has nothing else to do but lie on his mat, drink European *Kava*[20] and burn smoke rolls. He gives away the finished boats for more round metal and heavy paper, even though others worked for his money.

Then the people say: "He is rich." They envy him, flatter him and say beautiful words to him. For the worth of a man in the white world lies not in his honor or in his courage or in the splendor of his reasoning, but in the amount of his money, how much money he can make each day and how much he

---

20 Kava is Samoa's national drink; European Kava is presumably alcohol. [PCC]

keeps in his thick iron trunk, which not even an earthquake can destroy. There are many whites who save up money made for them by others, then bring it to a place which is well guarded. They keep bringing more until one day they will no longer need workers for themselves, because now the money works for them all by itself. How this is possible without magic I have never learned; but it is the truth that money constantly grows, like leaves on a tree and that the man who has it gets richer, even as he sleeps.

Now, if a person has a lot of money, much more than other people, so much that a hundred, even a thousand others could make their work lighter for themselves—he still gives them nothing. He lays his hands on the round metal and sits on top of his heavy paper with greed and self-satisfaction gleaming in his eyes. And if you ask him: "What do you want to do with your money? What more can you do on earth than to clothe yourself, eat and still your thirst?," he knows not what to say or he replies: "I want to make even more money. Always more. And more again." And you soon recognize that the money made him so sick, that all his senses are possessed by money.

He is sick and possessed, because he hitches his soul to the round metal and the heavy paper and can never have enough or stop gathering even more. He cannot reason like this: "I want to leave this world without complaint or injustice, just as I came here, because the Great Spirit sent me to earth without the round metal and the heavy paper." Only very few consider this. Most stay with their sickness and never regain the health of their heart. They rejoice in the power which gives them all their money. They swell in their conceit like rotten fruits in the rain. They feel gratified to leave their brothers to their raw, hard work, so that they can grow fat in their body and prosper. They do this and yet their conscience doesn't suffer. They look with satisfaction at their beautiful pale hands, which will never again be soiled. That they steal the energy off others and add it to theirs does not despair them, nor does it rob them of their sleep. They don't think of giving others a part of their money or to make their work easier for them.

Thus, there is a half of Europe which must do hard and dirty work, while the other half works little or not at all. The one half has no time to sit in the sun; the other half plenty. The *Papalagi* says: "not all humans can have the same amount of money and sit in the sun at the same time." From this teaching he takes the right to be cruel, for the sake of money. His heart is bitter and his blood is cold; he is insincere, he lies, and he is always dishonest and dangerous when his hand grasps for money. How often a *Papalagi* slays another for the sake of money. Or he murders him with the venom of his words; he uses his words to intoxicate him, in order to rob him. That is why no one trusts the next person, because all know of each others' weakness. That is why you can never tell whether a man who has a lot of money is good in his heart; what is certain is that he can be very evil. You never know how and from where he has taken his treasures.

But then, the rich man never knows whether the honors, which are offered him, are because of him or his money. Mostly, they are because of his money. That is why I cannot understand the shame of those who don't have much round metal and heavy paper. Instead of envying the rich man, they should let themselves be envied. Just as it is not considered good or proper to carry a large burden of shells, so it should be with the burden of money. It takes the breath away from man and robs his limbs of their freedom.

But the *Papalagi* does not want to do without money. No one does. He who doesn't love money is ridiculed, is *valea*[21]. "Wealth—having a lot of money—makes happy," says the *Papalagi*. And: "The land which has the most money is the happiest." My enlightened brothers, we are all poor. Our land is the poorest under the sun. We don't have enough round metal and heavy paper to fill but one trunk. We are impoverished beggars in the thoughts of the *Papalagi*. And yet! When I look at your eyes and compare them with those of the *alii*, I find theirs pale, wilted and tired, but yours are alive like the great light, gleaming with joy, strength, life and health! Only with the children of the *Papalagi* did I

[21] Stupid

see eyes like yours, before they could speak, when they still knew nothing of money. How the Great Spirit must have favored us, to protect us from the *aitu*. Money is an *aitu*, because all money does is evil and makes evil. He who touches money is caught in its magic, and he who loves it must serve it and must give it all his strength and his joy, as long as he lives. Let us praise our custom to despise the man who charges for his hospitality or who demands an *alofa*[22] for each fruit he hands out. Let us praise our custom which does not tolerate that one man has a lot more than the other, or that one man has a lot and another nothing. This way our hearts will not become like that of the *Papalagi,* who can be happy and cheerful, even when his brother next to him is saddened and despondent.

Above all other things, let us be careful of money. The *Papalagi* holds out the round metal and the

---

22 Gift, a payment

heavy paper to make us covet it. It shall make us richer and happier, he says. Already, many of us are blinded and have gotten the sickness. But if you heed the words of your humble brother, knowing that I speak the truth when I tell you that money never makes happier or brings more joy, but brings to the heart and the whole man a dreadful confusion; that with money no man can really be helped or made feel more content, strong or happy—then you will hate the round metal and the heavy paper like your worst enemy.

How the many things make the Papalagi poor

This is how you recognize the *Papalagi*: he wants to convince us that we are poor and miserable and that we need much help and pity, because we don't have things. Let me report to you, my beloved brothers of the many islands, what this is, a thing. The coconut is a thing; the fly whisk, the loincloth, the shell, the ring, the eating bowl and the head gear—all these are things. But there are two types of things. There are things which are made by the Great Spirit, which we don't see being made and which cause human beings no work and cost them no effort, like the co-conut, the shell, the banana. Then there are things which are made by human beings, which make much work and cost much effort, like the ring for the finger, the eating bowl, or the fly whisk. These things made by the hands of man are the things the *alii* be-lieves we lack; he cannot mean that we lack the things of the Great Spirit. Indeed, who is richer and who has more things of the Great Spirit than we? Let your eyes wander, let them wander afar to where the rim of the earth holds up the great blue dome. All is full of the great things: the forest with its wild pigeons, its hummingbirds and parrots; the lagoon with its sea cucumbers, its shells, its crayfish and the other creatures of the sea; the beach with its bright face and the soft fur of the sand; the great water, which can rage like a warrior and smile upon us like a *taopou;* the great blue dome, which changes each hour and bears blossoms which give us light of gold and silver.

Why should we be foolish and make more things beyond these things of the Great Spirit? We could never rival him, because our mind is too small and too weak when measured against the power of the Great Spirit, and our hand is much too frail compared to his mighty great hand. Whatever we can do is only modest and is not worthy of talk. We can lengthen our arm by wielding a club; we can enlarge our hand by holding a *tanoa*[23]; but no Samoan and no *Papalagi* has ever made a palm tree or the trunk of a *kawa*. But the *Papalagi* believes that he can make such things, that he is as strong as the Great Spirit. Thousands and thousands of hands do nothing from sunrise to sunset but make things. Human things, whose purpose we don't know and whose beauty we cannot understand. And the *Papalagi* thinks of more and more things. His hands work feverishly, his face turns grey as ash and his back is bent; but he alights with happiness when he can make new things. At once, all others want to have the new thing, they worship it, they place it in front of them and they sing about it in their language.

Oh, my brother, if you could believe me: I have uncovered the thoughts of the *Papalagi* and I have seen his will, as clearly as if the noonday sun had lit

[23] A wooden bowl in which the national drink is prepared

it. Because he crushes the things of the Great Spirit, wherever he goes, he wants to bring back alive that which he destroyed, from his own strength. In this way he convinces himself that he is the Great Spirit, because he makes many things.

Imagine, brothers, if a great storm came in the next hour and took the forest and its hills, its leaves and its trees with it; if it took all the shells and the creatures of the lagoon; if there were no longer a hibiscus flower to adorn the hair of our maidens—if everything, everything we see were gone, only the sand were left, and the earth resembled a flat hand or a hillside covered with lava. How we would weep for the palm tree, the shell, the forest and everything else. Now, where the many huts of the *Papalagi* stand, in the places they call towns, the land is empty as a flat hand, and this is why the *Papalagi* became demented and played the Great Spirit, so that he could forget what he didn't have. Because he was so poor and his land so desolate, he grasped for things and collected them, like the fool who collects wilted leaves and fills his hut with them. That is why he envies us and wishes that we should be as poor as he is.

There is great poverty where a man needs many things; he proves that he is poor in the things of the Great Spirit. The *Papalagi* is indeed poor, because he is possessed by things. He can no longer live without things. When he makes a tool out of the back of a turtle, so that he can comb his hair after oiling it, he goes on to make a skin for his tool, then for the skin a small box, then for the small box a large box. He places everything in skins and boxes. There are boxes for loincloths, for outer cloths and inner cloths, for wash cloths, for mouth cloths and other cloths; boxes for hand skins and foot skins, for the round metal and the heavy paper, for food and for the holy book, for everything. When he makes a thing, he goes on to make many where one would suffice. If you go to a European cook house, you see so many eating bowls and cooking tools as will never be needed. And for each meal there is a different *tanoa,* one for the water and another for European *kawa;* for the coconut a different one than for the pigeon.

One European hut has so many things that, even if a whole Samoa village loaded the hands and arms of every man and woman, the whole village could still not carry it all. In one hut there are so many things that the white chiefs need many men and women to do nothing but put back all the things where they belong and clean the sand off them. Even the most elevated *taopou* spends much time to count her things, move them around and clean them.

Brothers, you know I do not lie to you and I say the truth about all that I have seen, nor do I add things or take away from them. So, believe me, there are people in Europe who hold the firestick at their head and slay themselves, because they will die before going on living without things. For the *Papalagi* has intoxicated his mind in many ways, and so he tells himself that he cannot live without things, just as a man cannot live without food.

That is why I have never found a hut in Europe, where I could lie well on my sleeping mat, where nothing would disturb my limbs when I stretched them. All the things around me sent lightning or screamed loudly with their tongues of color, so that I could not close my eyes. Nowhere could I find real rest and never did I long more for my hut in Samoa, where there are no things other than my mats and where nothing comes to me but the breeze from the sea.

He who has few things calls himself poor and mourns. There is no *Papalagi* who sings and has cheerful eyes if he only has a sleeping mat and an eating bowl, like each one of us. The men and women in the white world would complain in our huts, they would run to get wood from the forest and the backs of turtles; glass, wire and colored stones and much more would move their hands from morning to night, until their Samoa hut would be filled with small and large things. Things, which easily crumble, which can be destroyed by any fire or any rainstorm, so that new things will have to be made all the time.

The more a man is a real European, the more things he will need. That is why, in making things, the hands of the *Papalagi* never rest. That is why the face of the white man is often so tired and sad, and that is why only few white men recognize the things of the Great Spirit and only few play in the village square, make up verses, or sing, or dance in the light, so that they may take joy in their limbs as we are all meant to do.[24] They have to do things. They have to guard their things. The things hang on to them and crawl on them like small sand fleas. With cold heart, they commit any crime to get things. They make war on one another, not for honor or to measure their strength, but for the sake of things.

But, despite that, they must recognize the great poverty of their life, or there would not be so many *Papalagi* who enjoy high honors for spending their lives pushing hairs into colorful juices, in order to throw splendid mirror images onto white mats. They write down all the beautiful things of God, as colorful and happy as they know to do. They also make human forms of earth; they make them without cloths, or in the image of a maiden with the

---

24 The Samoan villagers often meet to play together or to dance. Dancing is popular from the earliest youth on. Each village has its own songs and its own poet. In the evening, the sound of singing comes from each hut. Because the language is rich in

graceful, free movement of the *taopou* of *Matautu*[25],
or the figures of a man swinging a club or stretching
a bow or looking up, as if watching for a pigeon in
the trees. To some of these humans made of earth,
the *Papalagi* build especially large ceremonial huts,
where people will come from afar to enjoy their holi-
ness and beauty. They stand in front of these figures, tightly wrapped in their many loincloths, and
they shudder. I have seen the *Papalagi* cry with joy
when beholding such beauty, beauty which he himself has lost.

Now the white man wants to bring us his treasure,
so that we should become rich, too—his things. But
these things are nothing but poisonous arrows, from
which he dies whose chest is struck. "We must force
needs upon them," I heard a man say who knows
our land well. Needs are things. "Then, they will be
willing to work," the clever man then said. By this,

vowels and the islanders have an unusually developed sense of sound, the effect is
particularly charming. [ES]
25 Village on the island Upolu

he thought that we should also give the strength of our hands to make things; things for us, but mainly things for the *Papalagi*. We, too, should become tired, grey and bent.

Brothers of the many islands, we must be vigilant and have an alert mind, for the words of the *Papalagi* are like sweet bananas, but they are filled with secret spears which want to take away all the light and joy within us. Let us never forget that we need only few things, other than the things of the Great Spirit. He gave us the eyes with which to see his things. And the span of more than one human life is needed to grasp them all. And never has a greater lie come from the lips of the white man than this— that the things of the Great Spirit are without merit and that his own things are of greater use and value. His own things, of which there are so many, and which blind us and sparkle and often wink at us and try to entice us, have never made a *Papalagi's* body more beautiful, or his eyes more joyful, or his reasoning stronger. That is why his things are of no use, and what he tells us and wants to push upon us is of evil spirit, and his thought is drenched with poison.

HOW THE PAPALAGI IS WITHOUT TIME

The *Papalagi* loves the round metal and the heavy paper; and he loves to drink much liquid made from fruit; and to put meat from slain pigs and cows and other monstrous animals into his belly. But above all things, he loves what cannot be held but is still there—the time. He makes much commotion and foolish talk about it. Even though there cannot be more of it than what fits between sunrise and sunset, he is still not satisfied.

The *Papalagi* is always dissatisfied with his time, and he complains to the Great Spirit that he has not been given more of it. He tempts God and his great wisdom in that he divides up each day after a certain plan, and then divides it further. He cuts up his day as one would cut up a soft coconut into small squares. All parts have their name: second, minute, hour. The second is smaller than the minute, which is smaller than the hour. Together they make up an hour, and one has to have sixty minutes and many more seconds before one has enough to make an hour. This is an intricate matter, which I never fully understood, because it makes me dizzy to think longer than necessary about such childish matters. But the *Papalagi* makes a great body of learning out of it. The men, the women, and even children who can hardly stand on their own legs, carry in their cloth, or fastened to thick metal chains hanging from their neck, or tied to their wrist with a piece of hide, a small, flat, round machine from which they can read the time. This reading of time is not easy. One practices with children by holding the machine to their ear to entice them.

Inside this machine, which can easily be carried on two fingers, it looks like the belly of the large ships, which you have seen. But there are much larger and heavier time machines, as well, which stand inside the huts or hang below the highest roofs, so that they can be seen from afar. When part of the time is gone, little fingers outside the machine show this, while the machine screams and its spirit strikes against the iron in its heart. Yes, there is a tremendous noise in a European town when part of the time has gone.

When this time noise happens, the *Papalagi* complains: "It is a heavy burden that another hour has passed." Then, he makes a sad face, like a man who has to bear much suffering, even though a new hour has just arrived. I have never understood this, but I think that it may be a burdensome sickness. "The time eludes me!"—"The time runs like a horse!"—"Give me a little time!"—these are the complaints of the white man.

Here is why I say this could be a sickness: Assume that the white man is inclined to do something which his heart desires; he might want to go into the sunshine, or take his canoe down the river or be in love with his maiden— most of the time, he will spoil his desire by clinging to the thought: "I was not given time to be merry." The time is there, but no matter how hard he tries, he cannot see it. He names a thousand things which take time from him, bends over his work, complaining and sullen, even though he has no fresh air and doesn't love his work, and even though no one forces him to do it, except he himself. But if he suddenly sees that there is time, that it is still there, or if another man gives him time (the *Papalagi* sometimes give each other time and nothing is so highly esteemed as this), then he lacks the air, or he is too tired from his work and his joy is gone from him. And then he vows to do tomorrow what he has the time to do today.

There are *Papalagi* who say that they never have time. They run around without design, as if possessed by an *aitu,* and wherever they go they cause unhappiness and dread, because they have lost their time. This possession is a terrible condition, a sickness which cannot be healed by any medicine man and which spreads to other people and brings them misery. Because every *Papalagi is* possessed by this fear of his time, he knows exactly—and so does each woman and each small child—how many times the moon and the sun have risen, since he himself saw the great light for the first time. This is so important that it is celebrated with flowers and eating ceremonies, in certain spans of time which are of equal length. How often have I felt that others pitied me when I was asked how old I was and when I laughed and could not tell. "You have to know how old you are." I kept quiet and thought it was better if I did not know.

How old to be means how many moons to have lived. This counting and thinking is full of danger, because by doing so, the white man has recognized how many moons most people live. Now, every man pays attention and when many moons have passed for him, he says: "Now I must soon die." He loses his joy and soon dies.

There are in Europe only very few people who have time. Perhaps there are none at all. That is why most run through life like a rock thrown through the air. Almost all of them look down on the ground when they walk and throw their arms as far ahead of themselves as they can, to be able to move faster. When you stop them, they shout with impatience: "Must you disturb me? I have no time—see that you use yours better." They act as if a human who walks fast were better and braver than one who goes slowly.

I saw a man, whose head went silly, who rolled his eyes and opened his mouth wide like a dying fish, who turned red and green and beat around him with his hands and feet, only because his servant came a breath later than he had promised. This breath was a sizeable loss for him, which could never be forgiven. The servant had to leave his hut, because the *Papalagi* sent him away and shouted: "You have stolen enough of my time. A human being who does not respect time, is not worthy of it."

Only once did I meet a human being who had lots of time and did not complain, but he was poor and dirty and forsaken. No one went near him and no one respected him. I could not understand such behavior, because his walk was without haste and his eyes had a quiet, cheerful smile in them. But when I asked him, he lifted his brow and said sadly: "I never knew to use my time, which is why I am a dejected pauper." This man had time, and yet he was also unhappy.

The *Papalagi* uses all his strength and wastes all his thoughts on how he can make time as dense as possible. He uses water and fire, the storm, and the thunderbolt in the sky to stop time. He puts iron wheels under his feet and gives wings to his words to gain more time. And why all this effort? What does the *Papalagi* do with his time? I have never seen through this, although he always makes great words and gestures, as if the Great Spirit had invited him to a *fono*.

I think the time escapes him like a serpent a wet hand, because he tries to hold it too firmly. He doesn't allow it to come to him. He always chases behind it with hands stretched out and does not allow it to rest, to lie in the sun. Time should always be nearby and should sing or say something. But time is also quiet and peaceful and loves to rest and to spread out on the mat. The *Papalagi* does not know time, he doesn't understand it and that is why he mishandles it with his bad manners.

Oh, you beloved brothers! We have never complained about time. We have loved it as it came, have never chased it, have never tried to fold it together or cut it apart. Never did it bring us need or distress. He among us who doesn't have time, let him step forward! Each of us has much time; but we are happy with time, we don't need more of it than we have and we have enough. We know that we will still reach our goal early enough and that the Great Spirit will call us to him at his will, even if we don't know the number of our moons. We must free the poor, confused *Papalagi* from his illusion, we must give him his time back. We must break his little, round time machine and announce to him that there is more time between sunrise and sunset than any human being can use.

HOW THE PAPALAGI HAS MADE GOD POOR

The *Papalagi* has a peculiar way of thinking, which is most confused. He always looks for something that is to his benefit and makes him look right. Thus, he mostly thinks of one man and not of all human beings. And this one man is himself.

When a man says: "My head is mine and it is no one else's but mine," then this is so. This is really so and no one can disagree with it. And, in the same way, no one has more claim to his own hand than he whose hand it is. Up to this point I can agree with the *Papalagi*. But now he also says: "This palm tree is mine," because it stands in front of his hut. Just as if he himself had made it grow. But the palm tree is never his. Never. It is God's hand, and he extends it towards us out of the earth. God has a great number of hands. Each tree, each flower, each leaf of grass, the sea, the sky, the clouds—all these are hands of God. We may reach for it and take joy in

it; but we must never say: God's hand is my hand.
But this the *Papalagi* does.

In our language, *lau* means "mine" and it also
means "yours"; it is one and the same thing. But in
the language of the *Papalagi* there are no two words
which are more different than "mine" and "yours."
Mine is what belongs to me and to me alone. Yours
is what belongs only to you alone. That is why the
Papalagi says of everything which stands in the
vicinity of his hut: "It is mine." No one has a right to
it but he himself. Wherever you go and wherever
you see something of the *Papalagi*, a fruit, a tree, a
creek, a forest or a heap of earth—always is there
someone nearby, who says: "This is mine. Don't
touch what is mine!" If you still reach for it, he will
shout, call you a thief, which is a word of great
shame, and this because you dared touch the
"mine" of another. His friends and the highest

chief's servants will come running to put chains on
you and bring you to the *fale pui pui* and you will be
despised for your whole life. So that no one reaches
for the things which he has declared as his own,
what belongs or doesn't belong to a man will be
written down in special laws. And there are people
in Europe who do nothing but watch out that no
one ignores these laws, so that a *Papalagi* does not
lose anything which he has taken for himself. In this
way, the *Papalagi* wants to give the impression that
he has a real right to a thing, as if God had given
him his things for all time. As if the palm tree, the
flower, the sea, the sky and the clouds really be-
longed to him.

The *Papalagi* must make such laws and have such
guardians of his many "mines," so that others, who
have only little or no "mine," cannot take anything
from him. Because where many take much for them-

selves, there are also many who have nothing in their hands. Not everyone knows the tricks and the secret signs which lead to much "mine" and a special kind of bravery is needed, which does not always get along with what we call honor. It is possible that those who have little in their hands, because they don't want to offend God and steal from him, are the best *Papalagi*. But I am sure there are not many of them.

Most take from God without shame. They don't know any other way. They often don't even know that they are doing something evil, because everyone does it and no one thinks much about it or feels remorse. Many receive their "mines" when they are born, from the hands of their father. It is clear that God has hardly anything left; the human beings have taken almost everything from him and have made it into their "mine" and "yours."

Because some get more than others, there is not sunshine for everyone, even though the sun is made for all. But in the large sunny spots there are often only a few, while the many who have to stay in the shade, are deprived of sun. Surely, God cannot be happy when he is no longer the highest *alii sili*[26] in his great hut. The *Papalagi* denies him in that he says: "All is mine." But this far he does not think, even if he is thinking all the time. On the contrary, he declares his doings as honest and righteous. But before God he is dishonest and unrighteous. If he thought right, he would know that nothing belongs to us that we cannot hold firm. That we cannot hold on to anything. He would understand that God gave us a great place, so that there would be enough room and enough joy for all of us; so that there would be a sunny spot and a little pleasure for each of us; so that each human being would have a small stand of palms and a small place for his feet to stand on. That is how God wants it and how he decided it. How could God forget even one of his children? And yet, so many are searching for the small spot which God has left for them.

Because the *Papalagi* cannot hear the laws of God and makes his own laws, God sends him many enemies to attack his things. He sends him the water and the heat to destroy his "mine," and decay and rot. He also gives power over his treasures to the fire and the storm. But mostly he places fear in the soul of the *Papalagi*. The *Papalagi* can never sleep deeply, because he must be on guard that the things which he gathered in the daytime are not carried away at night. He must always keep his hands and his reason attached to his "mines." And how all the "mines" always torment him and mock him and say: "because you took me from God, that is why I pain you and cause you much grief."

But God has given the *Papalagi* an even worse punishment than his fear. He gave him the fight between those who have only a small "mine" or none at all, and those who call a large "mine" their own. This fight is hot and heavy and carries on day and night. It is the fight which all suffer and which takes the joy of life from all. Those who have should give, but they don't want to part with anything. Those who have nothing want to have, but get nothing. Yet they, too, are rarely God's children. They only came too late to the robbery, or were not skillful, or did not have the opportunity. That God is the victim, only very few realize. And only very seldom can one hear the call of the just man, that all should be given back into God's hands.

Oh, brothers, how do you think about a man who has a hut large enough for a whole Samoa village and will not give the stranger a roof for the night?

How do you think about a man who holds a bunch of bananas in his hands and will not give a single fruit to him who starves and is begging? I see anger in your eyes and great contempt on your lips. Think thus: this is the way of the *Papalagi* at every moment. And if he has a hundred mats, he will not offer one to him who doesn't have a mat. Instead, he will blame the other and make him feel guilty, because he doesn't have a mat. He may have his hut full of food stores up to the highest peak of his roof, more than he and his *aiga* can eat in many years, but he will not go and search for the ones who have nothing to eat and who are pale and hungry. And there are many *Papalagi* who are pale and hungry.

The palm tree yields its leaves and fruit when they are ripe. The *Papalagi* lives like a palm tree which wants to keep its leaves and fruits: "They are mine! You cannot have them or eat from them!" How should the palm tree ever bear new fruits? The palm tree has much more wisdom than the *Papalagi*.

Among us, too, there are many who have more than others and we do honor to our chief, who has many mats and pigs. But this honor only goes to him alone and not to the mats and the pigs. Because these we gave him as *alofa,* to show him our joy and praise his great courage and wisdom. But the *Papalagi* admires the mats and pigs of his brother and cares little for his courage or wisdom. A brother without mats and pigs has only very little honor, or none at all.

Since the mats and the pigs cannot themselves go to the poor and the hungry, the *Papalagi* cannot see a reason to bring them himself. Because he does not respect others, but only their mats and their pigs, he keeps them for himself. If he loved and

honored his brothers, and if he were not fighting
with them over the "mine" and "yours," he
would bring them mats, so that they could
rejoice in his great "mine." He would share his own
mat with them, instead of pushing them into the
dark night.[27]

But the *Papalagi* does not know God gave us the
palm tree, the banana, the delicious taro fruit, all
the birds of the forest and all the fish of the sea, so
that we should enjoy them and be happy. Not only
to a few among us, while others wane and suffer. If
God held out his hand to one man, he must pass it
on to the next, so that the fruit in his hand will not
wither. For God reaches his many hands to all human beings; he does not want that one has more
than the other or that one may say: "I stand in the
sun, you belong into the shade." We all belong in
the sun.

27 Tuiavii's disrespectful words about our property rights become more understand-
able in the context of Samoa's system of complete communality of ownership.
The concept of "mine" and "yours," as we know it, was truly unknown. On all my
travels, the natives always shared their roof, their mat and their food with me. And

Where God holds all in his just hand, there is no fight and no need. The treacherous *Papalagi* is now trying to tell us, too: "Nothing belongs to God! What you can hold in your hands is yours!" Let us close our ears to such weak words and hold on to our good knowledge: all belongs to God.

often a chief would greet me with these words: "What is mine is yours." The concept of "stealing" is alien to any islander. Everything belongs to everyone. Everything belongs to God. [ES]

WHY THE GREAT SPIRIT IS STRONGER THAN THE MACHINE

The *Papalagi* makes many things, which we cannot understand , which we will never grasp, which weigh like heavy stones in our head. Things, for which we do not long, which can paralyze the weak among us and cause them to feel inferior. Therefore, let us view the wonderful arts of the *Papalagi* without being timid.

The *Papalagi* has the strength to make everything into his spear and into his club. He takes for himself the wild thunderbolt, the hot fire and the fast water and uses them against their will. He incarcerates them and gives them orders. They obey. They become his strongest warriors. He knows the secret of how to make the thunderbolt even more blinding, to make fire even hotter and the fast water even more rapid.

The *Papalagi* appears truly to be the one who breaks through the sky[28], the messenger of God, for

---

28 Papalagi means the white man, the stranger, but literally translated it means "he who breaks through the sky." Apparently, the first white missionary landing in Samoa arrived in a sailboat. The natives looked on from afar and mistook the

he rules the sky and the earth at his pleasure. He is fish and bird and worm and horse all the same. He bores into the earth. Through the earth. Below the widest rivers. He slips through mountains and rocks. He puts iron wheels under his feet and chases faster than the fastest horse. He climbs into the air. He can fly. I saw him glide through the sky like a seagull. He has the great canoe to ride on top of the water, and he has a canoe to ride under the water. He rides in a canoe from cloud to cloud.

Beloved brothers, I swear to the truth and ask you to believe your servant, even if you have doubts about what I report. For great and most admirable are the things of the *Papalagi* and I fear there are many among us who will become weak when confronted with such strength. And where should I start if I were to report all that my eyes beheld with great awe?

gigantic sail for a hole in the sky, through which the white man had come to see them. He broke through the sky. [ES]

You all know the great canoe which the white man calls the steamship. Is it not like a large, immense fish? How is it possible that he can ride from island to island faster than the strongest of our young men can paddle in a canoe? Did you see the large tail fin when the vessel moves forth? It moves exactly like that of the fishes in the lagoon. This large fin pushes the great canoe forward. How this is done is the great secret of the *Papalagi*. The secret rests in the belly of the great fish. There is the machine which gives strength to the large fin. Thus, it is the machine which harbors the strength. To describe to you what a machine is, the strength of my head is not sufficient. I only know this: it eats black rocks and in return gives its power. A power which a human being can never have.

The machine is stronger than the strongest weapon of the *Papalagi*. Give it the sturdiest *ifi* tree in the forest—the hand of the machine can break its trunk, as a mother breaks a taro fruit for her children. The machine is Europe's great magician. Its hand is powerful and never tires. When it wants to, it cuts hundreds, even thousands of strong *tanoes* in a single day. I watched it weave loincloths, as fine as if they were woven with the most delicate hand of a maiden. It wove from morning to night. It spat out a large mountain of loincloths. Shameful and deplorable is our strength when compared with that of the machine.

The *Papalagi* is a magician. Hum a song and he will catch this song and give it back to you, at any hour you desire to have it[29]. He holds a glass plate in front of you and catches your image on it. And a thousand times can he take your image from this plate, as many times as you may wish for it[30]. But even greater miracles did I behold than these. I reported to you

[29] Early sound recording systems were pioneered in the late 1800s. [PCC]
[30] Photographic experiments date back to the 18th century. By 1900, "roll film," as invented by George Eastman, was widely available. [PCC]

that the *Papalagi* snares the thunderbolts from the sky. This is truly so. He snares them, the machine must devour them, bite them to pieces and, then, at night, it spews them out in the form of thousands of small stars, fire flies and tiny moons[31]. It would be easy for him to cover our islands with light during the night, so that they would be bright as in the daytime. Sometimes, he releases the thunderbolts from his own use; he orders them on their way and gives them instructions for his distant brothers. And the thunder-bolts obey and take the instructions with them.

The *Papalagi* has strengthened all his limbs. His hands reach across the seas and to the stars and his feet are faster than wind and waves. His ear notices every whisper in *Savaii* and his voice has wings as a bird. His eye can see at night. It can see through you, as if your flesh were clear like water, and it can see every speck on the bottom

---

[31] The cities visited by Tuiavii were brightly lit by electricity at the turn of the century. [PCC]

of this water[32]. What I witnessed and what I now
report to you is but a small part of what my eye
was allowed to behold. And, believe me, the ambition of the white man is great, so that he wants
to create ever new and more powerful miracles,
and thousands sit diligently during the night and
think of how they could take a victory from God.
Because this is it: the *Papalagi* strives to be God.
He would like to crush the Great Spirit and take
his powers for himself. But God is still greater and
more powerful than the greatest *Papalagi* and his
machine, and he still decides who among us
should die and when. The sun, the water and the
fire still mostly serve him. And so far no white
man has determined the rise of the moon or the
direction of the wind according to his will.

As long as this is the case, these miracles mean little. And weak is he among us, beloved brothers,

32 X-ray technology was well underway by 1900. [PCC]

who submits himself to these miracles of the
Papalagi, who worships the white man, and who
views himself as inferior for the sake of the white
man's workings and because his hands and his mind
cannot achieve the same. Because as much as all
the miracles and achievements of the *Papalagi* daz-
zle our eyes—when viewed in the clearest light of
the sun, they mean less than the carving of a club or
the weaving of a mat, and resemble the play of a
child in the sand. For there is nothing that the white
man has created which can come even close to the
miracles of the Great Spirit.

Splendid and massive and adorned are the huts of
the high *alii*, which are called palaces, and more
beautiful yet are the high huts, which were erected
to honor God, which are often higher than the peak
of *Tofua*[33]. Yet, when compared to the hibiscus tree
with its fiery blossoms, to each frond of the palm

[33] High mountain on Savaii

tree, or to the richness of color and form of the coral forest, all this is coarse and raw and lacks the warm blood of life. Never yet has the *Papalagi* been able to weave a loincloth as delicate as the web which God weaves through the legs of each spider; and never can a machine be as fine and artful as the small sand ant which lives in our huts. The white man flies to the clouds as a bird, I say to you[34]. But the great seagull flies higher yet and faster than the human, and flies during storms. And its wings come from its body, while the wings of the *Papalagi* are a deception and can easily break or fall off.

Thus, all his miracles have a secret weakness, and there is no machine which does not need its guardian and its driver. And each machine hides within it a secret curse. For even when the strong hand of the machine does everything, while it works it also eats up the love which resides in each thing

---

[34] German inventor Otto Lilienthal made hundreds of flights in his gliders before the turn of the century. [PCC]

that is made with our own hands. What would a canoe or a club be worth if crafted by a machine, a bloodless, cold being, which cannot tell us of its work, cannot smile when it finishes and cannot carry things to its mother or father, so that they can be joyful, too. How should I love my *tanoa,* as I now do, if a machine could duplicate it at any moment, without my help? This is the great curse of the machine, that the *Papalagi* no longer loves anything, because it can duplicate anything, at any time. He must feed it from his own heart, to keep receiving its miracles, which are without love.

The Great Spirit wants to rule the powers of heaven and the earth himself and distribute them as he deems right. This is not for man to do. Thus, it is not without punishment that the white man attempts to make himself into fish and bird, into horse and worm. And much smaller is his gain than he admits to himself. When I ride through a village, I move faster; but when I walk, I see more and my friends call me into their huts. To come to a destination fast is rarely a real gain. The *Papalagi* always wants to be at his destination fast. Most of his machines serve only the purpose to get to a destination fast. When he reaches the destination, a new one calls him. Thus, the *Papalagi* chases through his life without rest; more and more he forgets how we can walk and stroll and move happily toward a destination which we don't seek, but which comes our way.

That is why I tell you: the machine is a beautiful toy of the great white children, yet with all its arts it must not frighten us. The *Papalagi* has yet to build a machine, which keeps him from dying. He has yet to do or build something that is greater than what God does and builds every hour. None of the machines and other arts and magic tricks have yet kept a human being alive, nor have they made a man more joyful and happy. Therefore, let us be guided by the wonderful machines and high arts of the Great Spirit and let us despise the games of the white God.

Of the Papalagi's Profession and How He Loses Himself in It

Each *Papalagi* has a profession. It is difficult to describe what this is. It is something which one should crave, but usually doesn't crave. To have a profession is this: always to do one and the same thing. To do something that can be done with closed eyes and without much effort. When I do nothing with my hands but build huts or weave mats—then building huts and weaving mats is my profession.

There are professions for men and for women. To wash cloths in the lagoon or to make foot skins shiny are the professions of a woman; to drive the steamship across the sea or to shoot pigeons in the forest are professions for men. The woman usually gives up her profession, as soon as she gets married, but the man only then begins to work at his profession with vigor. An *alii* will only give his daughter if her husband-to-be has learned a profession. A *Papalagi* without a profession cannot get married. Every white man should and must have a profession.

That is why every *Papalagi* must decide which work he desires to do for the rest of his life, long before he lets himself be tattooed as a young man. This is an important matter and the *aiga* talks about this as much as about what food they would like the next day. If he takes the profession of the mat weaver, then the old *alii* takes the young *alii* to a man who does nothing but weave mats. This man must now show the youngster how a mat is made. He must teach him so well that he can make a mat without looking. This may take a long time, but as soon as he can do it, he goes away from the man and people now say: "He has a profession." When later the *Papalagi* recognizes that he would prefer to build huts to weaving mats, people say: "He has missed his profession." This means the same as: "He has

shot past his target." This is a great anguish, because it is against custom to simply take another
profession. It is not honorable for the *Papalagi* to
say: "I cannot do this—I don't crave doing it"; or,
"My hands don't want to obey me."

The *Papalagi* have as many professions as there are
rocks on the lagoon. Of every pursuit they make a
profession. When a man gathers the wilted leaves of
the breadfruit tree, he has a profession. If he cleans
eating bowls, this is a profession, too. Everything
that can be done is a profession. With the hands or
with the head. It is also a profession to have
thoughts or to look at the stars. There is actually
nothing which could be done, out of which the
Papalagi will not make a profession.

Thus, when a white man says: "I am a *tussi tussi*[35],"
he does nothing but write one letter after another. He

---

35 Tussi = letter; tussi tussi = letter writer, scribe

doesn't roll out his sleeping mat on the floor, he doesn't go to the cook house to cook a fruit, he does not clean his eating bowls. He eats fish, but does not go fishing; he eats fruit, but never breaks a fruit from the tree. He writes one *tussi* after the other, because *tussi tussi* is his profession. Even though all of these things are professions, too: rolling out the sleeping mat, cooking fruit, cleaning eating bowls, catching fish or breaking fruit. But only the profession gives you the proper right to do these things. This is how it comes that most *Papalagi* can only do what is their profession, and even the highest chief, who has much wisdom in his head and much strength in his arm, cannot roll out his mat or clean his eating bowls. And this is how it also comes that he, who can write a colorful *tussi*, does not need to be able to paddle a canoe out of the lagoon, nor back. Thus, to have a profession means to only walk, only taste, only smell, only fight—only do one thing at all times.

In this doing-only-one-thing resides a great need and a great danger, because every man can end up in a situation where he has to paddle a canoe across the lagoon. The Great Spirit gave us our hands so that we can break fruit from the tree and pull the bulb of the taro fruit from the swamp. He gave them to us, so that we could protect our body against all enemies; and he gave them to us, so that we may rejoice in them at dance and play and do all other merry things. But he certainly did not give them to us so that we would only build huts, only break fruit, or only pull bulbs. Instead, they should be our servants and warriors at all times and on all occasions.

But this, the *Papalagi* cannot grasp. That his doings are wrong, completely wrong and against all the laws of the Great Spirit we can recognize in those white men who can no longer walk and put on as much fat in their lower body as a *puaa*[36], because

36 Swine

their profession makes them always rest; those white men who can no longer lift a spear or throw it, because their hand always holds the writing bone, as they sit in the shade and do nothing but writing *tussi;* those white men who can no longer ride a horse, because they always look at the stars or dig up thoughts from their heads.

Rarely can a *Papalagi* run or hop like a child, when he has reached manhood. When he walks, he drags his body through the air, as if he were hindered. He embellishes and denies this weakness by saying that walking, running and hopping are not proper and dignified things to do for a man. But this is only a hypocrisy, because his bones have become hardened and inflexible and all his muscles have lost their joy, because his profession banished them to sleep and death. The profession is an *aitu* which destroys life. An *aitu* which whispers nice things into a man's ear, but drinks the blood from his body.

But the profession harms the *Papalagi* in different ways, and it reveals itself as an *aitu* from yet another side. It is a joy to build a hut—to cut the trees in the forest and make them into posts, to then raise the posts, to put a roof over them and, in the end, when posts and beams and all other parts are well tied together with coconut fibers, to cover them with the dried foliage of the sugar cane. I don't need to tell you what joy it is when a village builds the hut of a chief and even women and children participate in the ceremony. Now, what would you say if only a few men from the village were allowed in the forest to cut trees and make them into posts? And these few would not be allowed to raise the posts, because their profession was only to cut down trees and make them into posts? And those who weave the roof could not help covering it with sugar cane leaves, because their profession was only to weave roofs? If not one of these men would be allowed to fetch the round pebbles from the beach to cover the floor with, because this was the profession of others yet? And only those could celebrate and initiate the new hut who live there, but not those who built it? You are laughing, and surely you will say: If we could only do one thing and could not do other things to help, for which we have the strength of a man, then we would have only half our joy, or none at all. And surely you would call a fool that man who would ask you to use your hand for only one thing, as if the other limbs and senses of your body were lame and dead.

This is what leads to the *Papalagi's* worst need. It is beautiful to go to the river to scoop water, once or even several times a day. But he who has to scoop water from sunrise to sunset, each day and during all hours, as long as his strength lasts and has to scoop again and again—he will finally throw the scoop from himself in anger to protest the shackles on his body. For nothing is so difficult for a human being but to keep doing the same thing at all times. There are even those *Papalagi* for whom scooping at the same source every day would be a great joy, but who are allowed to do nothing which is an effort or a joy, because they must only lift or lower their hand or push against a bar, and this in a dirty chamber, without light or sunshine. But their lifting or lowering or pushing against a bar is in the mind of the *Papalagi* still needed, because by doing it a machine may be moved or directed, which may cut cloth rings, chest shields, pant shells or other things. There are more people in Europe than palm trees on our islands, whose faces are ash grey, because they can find no joy in their work, because their work devours all their craving, because from their work comes no fruit, not even a leaf, in which they could take joy.

And that is why there is a glowing hatred in the men of all professions. Their heart resembles an animal that is chained, fights to free itself and still cannot escape. And, full of envy and resentment, all men measure their professions against each other. People speak of higher and lower professions, even though all professions are only a part of getting something done. For man consists of more than just hands, or feet, or a head; he is all of these things joined together. Hands and feet and head desire to be united. When all limbs and senses work together, then only can the human heart feel healthy joy, but never if only a part of the human is alive and the other parts are dead. This brings human beings confusion, desperation and sickness.

Because of his profession, the *Papalagi* lives in confusion. He will never recognize this, and surely,
if he heard me say these things, he would declare
me a fool for wanting to be a judge without knowledge, because how could I know, since I have myself never had a profession or worked like a
European. But the *Papalagi* has never brought us
the truth or the reason why we should work more
than God demands from us, so that we can be fed,
have a roof over our heads and take joy in the celebration in the village square. This work may seem
small and our lack of professions may seem great.
But he who is a proper man and brother of the islands, works with joy, not with anguish, or it is better not to work at all. And this is what makes us different from the white man. The *Papalagi* moans
when he speaks of his work as if he were crushed by
a large burden. But the young men of Samoa chant
when they walk to the taro fields, and the maidens

sing when they sit by the rushing creek to wash loin-cloths. Surely, the Great Spirit does not want us to become grey in a profession, or to drag ourselves along like toads or crawling insects in the lagoon. He wants us to stay proud and upright in all our pursuits, and he wants us to be human beings with joy in our eyes and limbs that are supple.

OF THE PLACE OF FALSE LIFE AND THE MANY PAPERS

Much would your servant have to tell you, beloved brothers of the great sea, to give you all the truth about Europe. To do that, my speech would have to be like a waterfall, which cascades from morning to evening, and still the truth would be incomplete, because the life of the *Papalagi* is like the sea, whose beginning and end cannot be beheld. It has as many waves as the great water; it rages and crashes, it smiles and dreams. And as no human could empty the seas with his hollow hand, I also cannot bring to you the great sea of all of Europe with my small mind.

Yet I don't want to forget to tell you this: as the sea cannot be without water, Europe cannot be without the place of false life and without the many papers. If you took these away from the *Papalagi,* he would resemble the fish which has been tossed by the surf onto the sand—he can only twitch with his limbs, but he can no longer swim and play. What is this place of false life? It is not easy to describe to you this place, which the white man calls "cinema," so that you can see it as with your own eyes[37]. In each village in Europe there is this mysterious place, which is loved by all human beings, more than the mission hut. Already the children dream and think about this place with longing.

The cinema is a hut, greater than the hut of the chief of *Upolu*, much greater. It is dark, even on the brightest day, so dark that no man can recognize the other—so that one loses one's sight when one enters and, even more so, when one leaves. Here, humans slip in and steal along the walls, until a maiden comes with a fire spark and takes them to where there is room. One *Papalagi* sits very close to another in the darkness, no one sees the other, the dark room is now filled with silent humans. Each one sits on a small board; all these boards point in the direction of the same wall.

---

[37] The original movie machine, the "kinetoscope," was patented in 1891. The silent movie era started in earnest in 1902, and ten years later, such classics as *Quo Vadis* and *Queen Elizabeth* hit the screen. In 1912, Italy, which sported the most proficient movie industry, had 717 films in production. [PCC]

From the bottom of this wall, as from a deep gorge, come loud sounds, and as soon as the eyes are used to the darkness, one recognizes a *Papalagi* who, in a sitting position, fights with a box. With stretched out hands he beats on a great number of small white and black tongues, which are pushed out by the box, and each tongue screeches loudly when it is touched, each in a different voice, so that a wild and insane disturbance is caused, as in a large village fight.

This noise is designed to divert our senses and make them weak, so that we believe what we see and don't doubt that it is real. For right in front of us, on the wall, there is now a ray of light, as if the moon threw a strong beam, and in this light there are human beings, real human beings, who are dressed and who look like real *Papalagi*, who move and walk back and forth, who run, laugh, jump, exactly the way it looks everywhere in Europe. It is like the mirror image of the moon in the lagoon. It is the moon and yet it is not, and, in the same way, this too is only an image. Everyone moves their mouth, hence, one does not doubt that they speak, and yet, one cannot hear a sound or a word, no matter how hard one listens and no matter how painful it is not to hear anything. And this is the main reason why the *Papalagi* beats his box so hard: he has to cause the impression that the people cannot hear because of his noise. And this is why writing signs appear on the wall, which tell what the *Papalagi* has said or what he will say.

Yet, these humans are false images, not real human beings. If one wanted to touch them, one would recognize that they are only made of light and cannot be grasped. They are only there to show the *Papalagi* all his joys and sufferings, his foolishness and his weaknesses. He can see the most beautiful women and men near him. Even if they are silent, he can still see their movements and the light in their eyes. They seem to look at him and talk to him. He observes the highest chiefs, with whom he can never meet, close up, as if he were their equal. He participates at large eating ceremonies, *fonos,* and other festivities, and he seems to be part of the eating and drinking and everything. But he also sees how a *Papalagi* steals the maiden from an *aiga.* Or how a maiden becomes unfaithful to her betrothed. He sees how a savage man grabs a rich *alii* at his throat, how his fingers dig deeply into the skin of the neck, how the eyes of the *alii* are pushed out, how he is dead and the savage tears the round metal and the heavy paper from his loincloth.

Now, as the eyes of the *Papalagi* behold such joy and such terror, he has to sit completely still; he is not allowed to scold the unfaithful maiden and may not run to the aid of the rich *alii,* in order to save him. But this does not pain the *Papalagi;* he looks upon this all with great delight, as if he had no heart. He senses no fear and no dread. He watches this all, as if he himself were a different being. When he watches, he always firmly believes that he is better than the human beings in the light beam, and that he himself would never commit the foolishness shown to him. He is quiet and holds his breath, while his eyes are fixed on the wall. But as soon as he sees a strong heart and a noble image, he draws it into his heart and says: "This is my image." He sits completely immobile on his wooden board and stares at the steep, straight wall on which nothing lives but the deceptive light beam, which is thrown by a magician through a small gap in the wall behind the *Papalagi.*

To draw into himself these small images, which do not have a real life, is what gives the *Papalagi* such great pleasure. In this dark chamber, he can place himself in a different life, without shame and without other people seeing his eyes. The poor can play the rich, the rich the poor, the sick man can think himself healthy and the weak man can be strong. Here, in the dark, every man can be in a false life, and live things which he has not lived and will never live in real life.

To give himself to this false life is a great passion for the *Papalagi;* it is often so great that he forgets his real life. The passion is a sickness, for a righteous man does not want to live a false life in a dark room, but a warm, real life in the bright sunshine. The consequence of this passion is that many *Papalagi* who come forth from the place of the false life can no longer tell the difference from real life and become confused, believe to be rich when they are poor; or beautiful when they are ugly. Or they do evil deeds, as they would not have done in their real life, but they do them now because they can no longer tell the difference between what is real and what is not. It is a similar condition as the one which you have seen when the white man has drunk too much European *kava* and believes to be walking on waves.

The many papers, too, cause the *Papalagi* to be faint and dizzy. What are they, the many papers? Think of a *tapa* mat, thin, white, folded and folded again, all sides covered with very narrow writing—these are the many papers or, as the *Papalagi* calls them, the newspaper. In these papers lies the whole wisdom of the *Papalagi*. He has to hold his head between them every morning and evening, to load it and make it full, so that he can think better and have much inside him, just as the horse runs better if it has eaten much fruit and its body if properly filled. Even before

the *alii* rises from his mat, messengers run throughout the country and hand out the many papers. It is
the first thing for which the *Papalagi* reaches, after he
thrusts the sleep from himself. He reads. He bores
his eyes into what is told by the many papers. And
all *Papalagi* do the same thing—they, too, read. They
read what the highest chiefs and the speakers of
Europe have said at their *fonos*. This is exactly written on the mat, even if it is something foolish that
they said. It is also written what cloths or skins they
wore, what these *alii* were eating, what the name of
their horse was, even if they suffered from sickness or
had weak thoughts.

In our land, what is told would sound like this:
"The *pule nuu*[38] of *Matautu* has this morning after a
good rest eaten the remainder of last night's *taro*;
then he went fishing and returned to his hut at
noon, where he lay on his mat and chanted and

read in the holy book until evening. His woman *Sina* first nourished her infant, then went bathing, and on her way home found a beautiful *pua* flower, with which she adorned her hair. Then she returned to her hut. And so on."

All that happens and what human beings do and not do, is written. Their evil and good thoughts are written, as is written whether they slaughtered a chicken or a pig or whether they built a new canoe. Nothing happens across the whole, wide land, which is not carefully told on this mat. The *Papalagi* calls this: "to be well informed about everything." He wishes to be informed about every-thing which happens from one sunset to the next in his land. He is upset if he misses something. He greedily takes it all into himself, even though terrible things and all that a healthy human mind would like to forget at once, are told along with all other things.

The terrible and hurtful things are often told more exactly than the good ones, in all detail, as if it was not more important and more joyful to tell of the good things.

When you read the many papers, you don't need to journey to *Apolima, Manono* or *Savaii* to know what your friends are doing, thinking or celebrating. You can lie on your mat quietly, because the many papers will tell you all. Now, this seems splendid and very comfortable, but it is an illusion. For when you now meet your brother and both of you have already held your head into the many papers, you will have nothing new or interesting to report to him. Because you both carry the same in your head, you are now silent or you will tell each other again what the many papers said. That is why it is always a stronger experience to be part of a celebration or a suffering yourself, than have it told from the mouth of a stranger and not having seen it with your own eyes.

But this is not what makes the many papers so bad for our mind, that it tells us what has happened. Instead, the many papers also tell us what we should think about this and that, about our high chiefs or the chiefs of other lands, and about the happenings and doings of people. The many papers want to make all people into one head; they fight your own head and your own thinking. They demand that each human being use the head and thoughts of the many papers. And in this they succeed. If you read the many papers in the morning you know at noontime what every *Papalagi* carries in his head and thinks.

The many papers are like a machine; they make new thoughts each day, many more than a single head could make. But most thoughts are weak thoughts without pride and power; they feed our head with nourishment, but they don't make it strong. We could just as well fill our head with sand. The *Papalagi* overfills his head with such useless paper nourishment. Before he can push one thought out of his head, he already takes another one in. His head is like the mangrove swamp, which suffocates in its own mud, in which nothing green and fertile can grow again, and where only vile fumes rise and stinging insects dwell.

The place of false life and the many papers have made the *Papalagi* what he is: a weak, lost human being who loves what is not real and can no longer recognize what is real; who holds the image of the moon for the moon itself and who believes a mat covered with writing is life.

OF THE SERIOUS SICKNESS OF THINKING

When the word "mind" comes over the lips of the *Papalagi,* his eyes stare at you intensely; he breathes hard and swells his chest like a warrior who has beaten his foe. Because this "mind" is something of which he is especially proud. Now, we are not talking about the powerful Great Spirit, who is called God by the missionary and of which we are all just a lamentable image; no, this is a little spirit, which belongs to the human and makes his thoughts.

If I can see from here the mango tree behind the mission chapel, it is not the mind that sees it because I only "see" it. But if I recognize it as taller than the mission chapel, then it is my mind that does this. Thus, I must not just see something, I must also know. This knowing the *Papalagi* exercises from sunrise to sunset. His mind is always like a loaded firestick or like a fishing rod ready to be cast. He pities us peoples of the many islands, because we don't practice knowing. Our mind is poor and therefore stupid like the animal of the wilderness.

Now, it may be that we spend little time practicing the knowing, which is called "thinking" by the *Papalagi*. But we should ask ourselves who is stupid, he who thinks not much or he who thinks too much? The *Papalagi* thinks at all times. My hut is smaller than the palm tree. The palm tree bends in the storm. The storm speaks with the great voice. This is how he thinks; in his own way, of course. But he also thinks about himself. My body is short. My heart is always cheerful when I see a maiden. I love to go on *malaga*. And so on.

Now, this is fine and good and may have some hidden value to someone who takes joy in this game within his head. But the *Papalagi* thinks so much that he has to think, needs to think, is even forced to think. He must think at all times. He finds it very difficult not to think and to live with his limbs as well. Often, he lives only in his head, and all his senses are in a deep sleep, even when he walks upright, talks, eats and laughs. The thinking and the fruits of his thinking—his thoughts—hold him captive. It is as if he were intoxicated by his own thoughts. When the sun shines beautifully, he thinks at once: "How nicely it shines!" He constantly thinks "How beautifully it shines!" This is wrong. Totally wrong. Foolish. For it is better not to think, when the sun shines. A clever Samoan stretches his limbs in the warm light and thinks nothing. He takes the sun not only into his head, but takes it also with both his hands, his feet, his thighs, his belly and all his body. He lets his skin and his limbs think for themselves. And surely they think also, even if in a different way than the head. But to the *Papalagi* his thoughts get into the way like a huge block of lava, which cannot be removed. He may think cheerful thoughts, but he doesn't smile; he may think sad thoughts, but he doesn't cry. He may be hungry, but he doesn't reach for the *taro* or the *palisami*[39]. He is a human being, whose senses live as enemies within his spirit—a human being who is split into two parts.

The life of the *Papalagi* often resembles that of a man who takes a canoe ride to *Savaii* and who thinks, as soon as he has pushed off the shore: "I wonder how long I will take to get to *Savaii*?" He thinks, but he doesn't see the appealing landscape along his way. Soon there is a hillside on his left. When he sees it, he cannot take his eyes from it. What could be behind the mountain? Could it be a deep bay, or a narrow one? His thoughts make him forget to chant along with the other youngsters, and he barely hears the teasing of the maidens. Hardly

39 A favorite Samoan dish

have the bay and the hillside passed, another thought torments him—whether there could be a storm before evening. Yes, whether there could be a storm. He scans the bright sky for dark clouds. He keeps thinking of the storm which could arrive. But the storm does not come and he reaches *Savaii* by nightfall unharmed. Yet to him it seems as though he had not made this journey, because all day long his thoughts were far away from his body and outside of the boat. He could just as well have stayed in his hut in *Upolu*.

This mind which tortures us so is an *aitu* and I cannot understand why I should love it. But the *Papalagi* loves and worships his mind and feeds it thoughts from his head. He never lets it go hungry and it doesn't distress him if the thoughts eat each other. He makes much noise with his thoughts and he lets them be loud like impolite children. He acts as though his thoughts are priceless like blossoms, mountains and forests. He speaks of his thoughts, as if the courage of a man or the cheerful nature of a maiden were not worth anything, when measured against it. He behaves as if there were a law some- where that human beings were forced to think much. When the palm trees and the hills think, they don't make much noise over it. And, surely, if the palm trees thought in as loud and fierce a way as thinks the *Papalagi*, they would not carry green leaves and golden fruits.[40] They would fall off, before ripening. But it is likely that they think very little.

There are many ways and methods to think and many targets for the arrow of the mind. Sad is the lot of those who think afar. How will it be when the next dawn turns the sky red? What will the Great Spirit intend with me, when I arrive in the *salefe'e*[41]? Where was I before the messengers of *Tagaloa*[42]

---

40 Tuiavii's note in brackets: [Because everyone knows that thinking makes people old and ugly in little time]. [ES]
41 Underworld
42 The highest of all gods

presented me with my *agaga*[43]? This type of thinking is as useless as if one tried to see the sun with closed eyes. It is not possible. In the same way, it is not possible to think into the far or back to the beginning. Those who try this, know. They sit from their childhood to their age like ice birds in one spot. They don't see the sun any longer, the wide sea, the lovely maidens; they see no joy, no emptiness, no nothing. They no longer enjoy even *kava* and at the dance in the village square their eyes are cast on the ground before them. They do not live, even though they are not dead. The serious sickness of thinking has befallen them.

This thinking is supposed to make the head great and high. When someone thinks much and fast, then they say in Europe he is a great head. Instead of being pitied, these great heads are especially honored. The villages make them chiefs, and wherever a

[43] The soul

great head goes, he has to think ahead of others, which gives everyone much pleasure and is much admired. When a great head dies, the whole land is in mourning and people wail about what has been lost. An image of the dead head is made of a rock and it is put in the market place for all to see. Yes, these stone heads are made even much larger than their true size in life, so that the people will admire them properly and will feel humbled by their own small head. Now, if you ask a *Papalagi* why he thinks so much, he will answer: "Because I don't want to stay stupid." Each *Papalagi* who does not think is considered *valea*[44], even if he is clever, or if he finds his way without thinking much.

But I believe this is only a pretense and that the *Papalagi* is driven by evil—that the real purpose of his thinking is to see through the powers of the Great Spirit. His way of doing this is described by

[44] Stupid

his noble sounding word: "knowing." To the *Papalagi,* knowing means to have a thing so close in front of your eyes, that it touches your nose or pushes through it. This pushing through and looking over all things is a tasteless and despicable obsession of the *Papalagi.* He takes the *skolopender,* cuts through its body with a tiny spear, pulls out his leg. How does a leg look without a body? How was it attached to the body? He breaks the leg to test its thickness. This is important; it is vital. He scrapes off a splinter, small as a speck of sand, and puts it under a long tube, which has magical powers and lets the eyes see much better[45]. With this large and strong eye he now examines everything, a tear, a piece of your skin, a hair, everything. He divides all these things until he gets to a point, where nothing can be broken and divided any longer. Although this point is always the smallest, it is the most vital, because it is also the opening to the

[45] Microscopes were in wide use in turn-of-the-century Europe. [PCC]

highest understanding, which is only possessed by
the Great Spirit.

But this opening is even barred to the *Papalagi* and
his best magical eye has not seen into it. The Great
Spirit will not allow his secrets to be taken. Never.
No man has ever wrapped his legs around a palm
tree and climbed higher than the tree is tall. At its
crest, he has to turn; there is no more trunk to go
higher. In the same way, the Great Spirit does not
like the curiosity of humans, which is why he has
wrapped long vines around everything, vines which
are without beginning or end. That is why everyone
who probes into too much thinking will surely find
out that at the end he is always stupid and that the
answers, which he himself cannot provide, must be
left to the Great Spirit. The most wise and coura-
geous of the *Papalagi* admit this. But most of those
who are sick with thought will not let their pleasure

go and that is why the path of thought leads a man so often astray—he is as one who ventures into the forest where no path has yet been tread. He gets confused and can suddenly not tell the difference between human and animal, as has actually happened. He says that a man is an animal and an animal human.

Terrible and fateful is it therefore that all thoughts, whether good or evil, are at once put onto white mats. "They are being printed," says the *Papalagi*. This means: what those sick ones think is now also written down by a machine, which is highly mysterious and full of wonders and which has thousands of hands and the strong will of many great chiefs. But not once or twice—thousands of times, endless times, always the same thought. Many of these thought mats are then pressed together in bundles. "Books," the *Papalagi* calls them, and to all parts of

the country they are sent. And these thought mats
are devoured like sweet bananas; they lie in each
hut, whole boxes are filled with them and old and
young eat at them, like rats nibble at sugar canes.
This is why so few can still think reasonably, in natural thoughts, as every righteous Samoan has them.

In the same way as many thoughts are pushed into
the heads of small children as fit in. They are forced to
devour their quantum of thought mats each day. Only
the healthiest push these thoughts away or let them
fall through their mind as if through a net. But most
overload their head with so many thoughts, that there
is no more room in it and no light can come in. This is
called "forming the mind" and the ongoing condition
of this widespread confusion is called "education."

Education means to fill one's head to the highest rim
with knowing. The educated one knows the length of

the palm tree, the weight of the coconut, the name
of all his great chiefs and the time of their wars. He
knows the size of the moon, the stars and all lands.
He knows every river by its name, each animal and
each plant. He knows everything, everything. Ask
the educated one a question and he shoots back an
answer before you have closed your mouth. His
head is always charged with ammunition; it is always ready to shoot. Every European gives the most
beautiful time of his life to make his head into a fast
firestick. Those who want to avoid this, are forced.
Every *Papalagi* must know, must think.

The only thing which could heal those who are sick
with thought—forgetting, throwing away thoughts—
is not practiced, which is why only very few can do
it. Most carry a heavy load in their head, so that
their body is tired from this burden and in time
becomes frail and wilted.

Should we now, beloved brothers, after everything that I have reported here in steadfast truth, imitate the *Papalagi* and learn to think like he does? I say no! Because we should not and must not do anything which does not make us stronger in body and happier and better in our spirit. We must guard against everything which may rob us of our joy of life; especially that which may darken our spirit and take away its bright light; especially that which may bring enmity between our head and our body. The *Papalagi* proves with his own example that thinking is a serious sickness, which makes the value of a human much smaller.

HOW THE PAPALAGI WANTS TO DRAW US INTO HIS DARKNESS

Dear brothers, there was a time when we all sat in darkness and none of us knew the strong light of the scriptures; when we ran around like children who could not find their hut and when our ears were deaf to the word of God.

The *Papalagi* has brought us the light. He came to us to free us from our darkness. He led us to God and taught us how to love God. That is why we honored him as the bringer of light, as the speaker of the Great Spirit, which the white man calls God. We recognized and accepted the *Papalagi* as our brother and did not bar him from our land, but shared all fruit and all edible things honestly with him, as we would do with our children.

No effort did the white man spare to bring us the scriptures, even when we acted like stubborn infants and resisted his teachings. For this effort and for all which he suffered for our sake, we must be thankful, pay homage to him forever and venerate him as our light bringer. The missionary of the *Papalagi* was the first to teach us about God, and he took away from us all our old gods which he called idols, because they did not have the true God in them. Thus, we stopped worshiping the stars of the night, the strength of the fire and the wind and turned towards his God, the Great God in heaven.

The first thing that God did was to take from us through the *Papalagi* all our firesticks and weapons, so that we could live peacefully among each other as good Christians. For you know the words of God, that we should all love each other and must not kill, this being his highest law. We gave our weapons and no wars have since devastated our islands, and one respects the other as his brother. We learned that God was right with his command, for today village after village lives in peace, where there was once disquiet and where terror did not want to take an end. And even if the great God has not yet filled each one of us with his love, we still recognize with gratitude that our spirit has grown greater and stronger, since we have worshiped him as the greatest chief and the ruler of the earth. With humility and thanks do we listen to his wise and great words, which make us steadily stronger in our love and which fill us more and more with his great spirit.

The *Papalagi,* I said, brought us the light, the heavenly light, whose flame lit our hearts and filled our spirit with joy and gratitude. He had the light earlier than we did. The *Papalagi* already stood in the light when the oldest among us were not yet born. But he holds the light only with his hand extended, to light the path for others; he himself, his body, stands in darkness and his heart is far from God, even though his voice calls for God, because he holds the light.

Nothing is more difficult and fills my heart with more sorrow, beloved children of the many islands, than to announce this to you. But we cannot guess wrongly about the *Papalagi*, lest he pull us into his darkness. He brought us God's word, yes. But he himself has not understood God's words and teachings. He has understood them with his mouth and with his head, but not with his body. The light has not penetrated him, so that he can reflect it and so that it can shine from his heart, wherever he goes— this light, which can also be called love. He no longer feels the falsehood which is in his words and in his body. But it can be recognized, because no *Papalagi* can any longer speak the word of God from his heart. His eyes become vacant when he tries, as if he were tired or the words did not mean much to

him. All whites call themselves children of God and
let their belief be written on mats by their chiefs. But
God is still distant to them, even if every one of
them has received the great teaching and knows of
God. Even those who are chosen to speak of God in
the splendid huts, which were built in his honor,
don't have God inside themselves, and their
speeches go to the wind and the great void. The God
speakers do not fill their speech with God; they
speak like the waves, which crash against the reef—
no one hears them any longer, even though they
rage without rest.

I can say this, without making God angry: we children of the islands were not worse when we prayed
to stars and the fire than the *Papalagi* is now. We
were lost in the darkness, because we did not know
the light. But the *Papalagi* knows the light and still
lives in darkness and is lost. The worst is that he

calls himself child of God and Christian; that he wants to make us believe that he is the fire, because he holds the flame in his hands.

The *Papalagi* rarely thinks of God. Only when a storm grasps him or a life is threatened, he remembers that there are powers above him and higher chiefs than himself. But on most days God is a disturbance to him and keeps him from his strange pleasures and joys. He knows that God would never like these and he also knows that if God's light were really within him, he would have to throw himself in the sand in shame. For nothing but hatred and greed and enmity fill him. Instead of being a light which banishes darkness and gives warmth, his heart has become a long, sharp hook—a hook destined for robbery.

Christian is what the *Papalagi* calls himself. A word like the most beautiful song: Christian. Oh, if we could only call ourselves Christians for all time. To be Christian means: to love the Great God and all your brothers, and then only yourself. Love—that is to do good—must be one and the same with us, as our blood, like our head and hand. The *Papalagi* carries the words Christian and God and love only in his mouth. He beats his tongue around and makes much noise. But his heart and his love are not bent before God, only before things like the round metal and the heavy paper, before thought of pleasure and of machines. No light fills him, but a fierce greed for time and for the foolish pursuit of his profession. Ten times will he go to the place of the false life, before he goes once to God.

Beloved brothers, the *Papalagi* has more idols today than we ever had—if an idol is that which people pray to, worship and carry as their most beloved thing in their hearts, next to God. The most beloved thing in the *Papalagi's* heart is not God. And that is why he does not serve God's will, but the will of the *aitu*. It is out of suspicion when I say the *Papalagi* may have brought us the scriptures in exchange for fruit and the largest and most beautiful part of our land. I believe he is capable of this, because I have discovered much filth and sin in the heart of the *Papalagi* and know that God loves us more than him, who calls us savage—a word which means a human who has the teeth of an animal, but no heart.

But God reaches into his eyes and tears them open so that he may see. He told the *Papalagi:* "Be as you must be. I shall no longer make you commandments." And the white man went and showed his true self. Oh, shame! Oh, terror! With thunderous tongue and with proud words he took our weapons and talked of God. Love each other. And now?

Oh, brothers, you must have heard the terrible reports, the godless, loveless and lightless events: Europe is slaying itself. The *Papalagi* has become deranged. One murders the one next to him. All is blood and horror and decay. The *Papalagi* is finally admitting it: I have no God in me. The light in his hand is dying. Darkness lies in his path—one can only hear the terrifying beating of the flying dogs and the screeching of the owls.

Brothers, love of God fills me and love for you, which is why God gave me my voice, so that I could tell you what I have told. So that we can find strength in ourselves and not fall victim to the quick and treacherous tongue of the *Papalagi*. Let us henceforth hold him off with our hands and call to him: "Be silent with your loud voice, as long as you don't show a joyful, strong face and clear eyes and as long as the image of God does not shine in you like the sun, your words are to us no more than the roaring of the surf and the rustling of the palm leaves."

And we should further swear that we will call this to him. "Stay away from us with your pleasures and joys; with your wild longing for riches in your hands and in your head; with your greed to be more than your brother; with your senseless doings; the confused things your hands make; your curiosity to think and to know, which still leaves you without knowledge. All your foolishness, which even makes your time on the mat restless."

For we don't need any of this and are satisfied with the noble and beautiful joys which God gave us in great number. May God help us, so that we are not blinded by the *Papalagi's* light and led astray, but that all paths are clear so that we can walk in his heavenly light and take it within us, which means to be good to each other and make much *talofa*[46] in our heart.

EPILOGUE

When I started working on the translation of Tuiavii's speeches, I knew almost nothing about Erich Scheurmann. But as my project progressed, there were times when his life and person became the focal point of my research.

My initial problem was that only the most sketchy details are available on Scheurmann. Out of the three most widely used German literary reference works, two merely compile the dates of his birth and death (1878–1957) and the publication of his more than twenty books. The third[1] contains a bibliography by Eckard Schuster, which is slightly more useful, but appears heavily biased. It details the young Scheurmann's art studies in Hamburg and his decision to join the *Wandervogel*[2] movement. His first two novels, which were modestly successful, appeared in 1911 and 1913. When he was 36 years old, in 1914, Scheurmann moved to Samoa, then a German colony. Later, he

---

[1] *Literatur Lexikon, Autoren und Werke deutscher Sprache,* Bertelsmann Lexikon Verlag, latest reprint 1991.

[2] Literally translated "wandering birds"; presumably a group of people devoted to seeing the world.

departed to the United States and stayed there until the end of World War I. Little is mentioned about the further course of Scheurmann's life, nor do any of his works, save the *Papalagi* and the author's two South Sea novels, merit any comment. To these works, however, the bulk of Schuster's bibliography[3] is devoted.

Paitea & Ilse, Scheurmann's first novel set in Samoa, is portrayed as contrasting decadent European civilization with romanticized South Sea lore. The bibliographer bemoans Scheurmann's "mental attitude" of elevating to central ideological themes concepts such as "purity," "race" and "nature," but fails to say what he means by this.

I was lucky enough to get hold of original copies of both of Scheurmann's early South Sea novels, *Paitea & Ilse* (1919) and *Erwachen* (1922) and found such criticism unfair and misguided. It is true that both novels

---

[3] Not to be mistaken with a biography. Schuster is one of many bibliographers who contributed to this encyclopedia of German literature; his summary of Scheurmann's life and works consists of less than 500 words.

contrast the path of civilization with the innocent existence of the South Seas, but Schourmann idealizes neither the natives, nor does he vilify the Germans who
find themselves disoriented in the Samoan island paradise. In *Paitea & Ilse*, the tragic figure is a young
German who marries an island girl and tries to mold
her childlike innocence into a goal-oriented, productive
existence. The novel's "knowing figure," the daughter of
a German plantation owner whom he befriends, cau-
tions against such an approach and instinctively under-
stands that such a transition cannot ever be successful,
but that innocence is a state of blissful perfection. There
is no happy ending to this story, nor is there to
Erwachen, which follows the same basic theme. I do
not understand Eckard Schuster's motive in casting
these novels in such a negative light. "Race" and "nature" are inherently necessary topics in any novel in-
volving as central characters both whites and Samoans,
set in an island paradise. Schuster does not say in which

way he believes Scheurmann makes "purity" a dominant theme or how the concept of purity is unreasonably used. If he refers to purity as a racist notion, which is the only negative connotation to the noun I can think of, he is intellectually dishonest. The only racial conclusion to which Scheurmann's plot points is that it is as improbable that a white man can abandon his goal-oriented upbringing, as it is that a Samoan islander can do without the support of a tribal community in which mythology and ritual are central. Of course, this is not to say that in today's "politically correct" world such logic would not meet with equally severe criticism.

The *Papalagi* does not fare better. We are told that Tuiavii's speeches are a satire, entirely made up by Scheurmann and that the author used Montesquieu's *Lettres Persanes*[4] as a model. But Montesquieu's work is full of original jest and *ésprit*, Schuster writes, while the *Papalagi* is filled with tedious stereotype.

---

4   The Baron de la Brède et de Montesquieu (1689-1755), a well known French philosopher and jurist, achieved literary success with this satirical work, which describes French society through the eyes of two imaginary Persian visitors to Paris.

Tedious and stereotypical? Beyond the obvious fact that Scheurmann's bibliographer was seriously prejudiced against his subject, it is difficult to contemplate how such misguided judgment could arise. One possibility is that Schuster merely glanced through Scheurmann's books and, in the case of the *Papalagi*, mistakenly convinced himself that it was meant to be a satire, before familiarizing himself with it. If this was indeed the case, he did an inexcusably poor job and thereby deprived a generation of potential readers of a most rewarding literary experience. A second potential reason for Schuster's harsh views is that he simply lacked in human quality and entirely missed the richness of both Scheurmann's compassionate writing style in his novels and the deep spirituality evident throughout Tuivaii's speeches, in which case he is to be pitied. Finally, it is possible that Schuster felt as insecure and uncomfortable about the topic of indigenous culture as did most of his peers at the turn of the century.

EPILOGUE

In this context, it is interesting to note how profoundly uncomfortable the British literary establish-
ment was with Robert Louis Stevenson's *South Sea
Tales*. Ill health forced Stevenson to travel the Pacific
and eventually settle in Samoa, where he died four
years later[5]. While there, he was expected to con-
tinue producing the historical romances which made
him famous—*The Master of Ballantrae, Kidnapped*
and *Treasure Island*. When his subject matter instead
turned to the daily life in distant colonies, London
reacted with disbelief. Oscar Wilde, who had asked
for some of Stevenson's writings to be sent to him
in jail had this to say when he received a copy of
the *Vailima Letters*: "I see that romantic surroundings
are the worst surroundings possible for a romantic
writer." Sidney Colvin, the famous literary critic who
was also Stevenson's editor, reacted even more neg-
atively. "I wish he had worked at anything else but
this," he wrote after reviewing *The Ebb Tide*, one of

[5] Stevenson died of a cerebral hemorrhage in 1894.

the stories which comprise the *South Sea Tales*. Reportedly, he even thought of ways to suppress Stevenson's South Sea works altogether, out of fear that it would damage Stevenson's reputation.

"Colvin's fears were unfounded," wrote Roslyn Jolly[6] in her splendid introduction to a recent reprint of the *South Sea Tales*. "*The Ebb Tide* did not damage Stevenson's reputation, because it was left out of the count by most critics when they came to reckon up Stevenson's achievements after his death. This was true not just of *The Ebb Tide*, but of all the South Sea tales. It was as if this body of work simply did not exist."

Why such paranoia? Partly, as Roslyn Jolly puts it, because "as early as 1889 Stevenson was drawing contrasts between native and expatriate society, in favor of the former." The stories were no longer romantic, but realistic; the venues were imaginary, but their plot was

---

6   Oxford University Press, 1996.

anchored in Stevenson's experience of contemporary Samoa. Roslyn Jolly tells us that this "led to accusations that Stevenson betrayed a 'prejudice against civilized men' and an 'indiscriminate love for Polynesians' whom he misguidedly romanticized." It is difficult for us today to understand how accounts as seemingly objective and accurate as Robert Louis Stevenson's written in the Pacific could so deeply offend the turn-of-the-century psyche. But we have to remember that imperialist society was driven by a sense of superiority and acted according to the principles of cultural dominance. In one of the *South Sea Tales* best known stories, *The Beach of Falesà*, Wiltshire, the one white character who does possess a sense of fairness and decency, captures it all when he muses: "They haven't any real government or any real law, that's what you've got to knock into their heads; and even if they had, it would be a good joke if it was to apply to a white man. It would be a strange thing if we came all this

way and couldn't do what we pleased." This attitude
was further compounded by the way imperialism was
portrayed back home. Government propaganda, literature and, lest we forget, the fastest growing medium
of the time, photography, all romanticized the English
role in the colonies.

In her introduction to the catalogue to the most important recent exhibition of photographs of turn-of-
the-century Samoa[7], co-curator Alison Devine
Nordström gives us a fascinating perspective of "the
kind of photographs of Samoa [which] interested the
West, as well as the means by which Westerners manufactured, transported, and consumed them. To our
knowledge, none was produced by a Samoan, and it
appears few were produced for Samoan consumption.
Because of this, these images are only minimally infor-
mative about the lives and realities of their subjects,
but can be extremely revealing of the people who

[7] "Picturing Paradise: Colonial Photography of Samoa, 1875 to 1925" was shown in
1996 in several American and European cities. Ms. Devine Nordström is Director
and Senior Curator at the Southeast Museum of Photography in Daytona Beach,
Florida.

'took' and used them." In short, as Alison Devine Nordström summarizes the situation, "These objects are artifacts of Western culture, and it is that culture which they reveal."

What they do reveal, incidentally, is highly descriptive of the distorted view in which turn-of-the-century Europeans saw themselves and the world around them. Invariably, the photographers from civilization established a stereotype that "defined non-Western people in terms of their differences from the culture controlling the image-making. Once the stereotype was established, information which contradicted it could be dismissed as anomalous, or otherwise ignored." For instance, a travel writer recollects how in 1890 John Davis, Apia's[8] first commercial photographer, described his choice of subjects the following way: "...though hundreds of native girls and youths presented themselves at his studio ... he was invariably able to choose

8 Samoa's principal town

only two, or three at most, who possessed the thick lips and sensual features which coincided with the stock European idea of the South Sea type."[9] Even worse, photographic images were frequently changed for Western audiences. Alison Devine Nordström tells us how this was done with a widely distributed photograph of a smiling young girl, which suddenly popped up in *Harper's New Monthly Magazine*. "The engraving, captioned 'The Merriest Sauciest Little Maid,' reinforces the stereotype of the available and compliant Polynesian woman by 'corrections' the engraver has made to the photograph, including the removal of the girl's upper garment. In its place, bare breasts have been drawn in, and her necklace of trade beads has been replaced with a more picturesque and exotic garland of flowers."

Predictably, such romantic notions were on a collision course with the disturbing insights which made up

---

[9] From Alison Devine Nordström's article; acknowledged source Safroni-Middleton

Stevenson's *South Sea Tales*. I must hasten to add that Stevenson took great pains not to romanticize the natives; some of them come across as foolish and greedy and, as a group, they are presented as humanly imperfect. But this did not mitigate the outrage many felt; what could not be forgiven is that Stevenson often depicts whites as the sources of evil and objects of revulsion.

Tuiavii's speeches, as well as Scheurmann's presentation of them, must have been viewed in imperial (and as of late colonialist) Germany in a similar way as were Stevenson's *South Sea Tales* in Victorian England. Is this part of the reason for the poor reception of the *Papapalgi* by Germany's literary institutions?

Whatever the answer may be, one nevertheless cannot ignore Eckard Schuster's assertion that Scheurmann may not be the true author of Chief

Tuiavii's speeches. Was Tuiavii merely a figment of Scheurmann's imagination? Or did Scheurmann take the essence of Samoan beliefs and dramatize them? Or was there really a Samoan Chief whose manuscript Scheurmann translated?

My first step in searching for the truth was to study the "time-lines" between Chief Tuiavii's speeches and actual events which occurred during this period. Scheurmann's travel dates and the way he describes his acquisition of the manuscript, caused me to assume that Tuiavii visited Europe around the turn of the century and worked on his notes there and after his return. In terms of technological advances, all dates match; inventions like the telephone, the X-ray machine, the motion picture and the submarine were indeed the sensation of the day. It is quite conceivable that Tuiavii had the chance to see them while visiting the continent. Yet, at the same time, such "miracles" were by no means commonplace and must have left a deep impression even on Europeans.

My next task was to consult Scheurmann himself. In reviewing all of his major writings, I found a discrepancy which greatly intrigued me. None of the author's major novels contains any preface, but the *Papalagi* does. In it, Scheurmann's sole purpose appears to be to explain his relationship with Tuiavii and how he came to make available the manuscript to European readers, in his own words "without the author's permission and surely against his will." How are we to understand such deliberations? As an expiation of Scheurmann's guilt over stealing a manuscript, or as an exceedingly clever way to make an invented tale more credible?

Here is how Scheurmann recollects what happened in Samoa in the preface to *Papalagi:* "Even though I lived well over a year in his immediate vicinity—I was a member of his village—Tuiavii only opened himself to me after we became friends, after he had gotten over my being European, or even forgotten it. Only after he had convinced himself that I was ready for his simple wisdom and wouldn't ridicule it (which I never did), only then did he let me hear fragments of his writings. He read them to me without any effort to impress, as if what he had to say was recorded history. But it was exactly through this way of relating that Tuiavii's observations came across to me with purity and clarity, so much so that I desired to record what I was hearing."

It was a long time before Tuiavii handed his manuscripts to his German friend and allowed him to translate them. Scheurmann emphasizes that this was to be solely for his personal use and not for any other purpose. All of Tuiavii's notes were unfinished and in need of more work. Only when his thoughts were clear on every point did he want to start his own "missionary work," as he called it. Scheurmann had to leave the South Seas before Tuiavii's goal was realized.

Erich Scheurmann's preface also contains some editorial commentary, which I find fascinating. He expresses concern that the "intuitive style" of Tuiavii's notes and some of "the breath of immediacy" conveyed by his manner of speech, will have been lost. He assures us that it was his ambition to translate literally and not to deviate from the original text or the order of its presentation. He hopes that he will be forgiven by those familiar with the difficulties of translating a "primitive language into German and to relate its childlike expressions without making them appear banal and stale." In this context, as well, Scheurmann's eagerness to come across as a diligent translator appears out of step with the theory that it was he who actually wrote the speeches.

Scheurmann ends his introduction by telling us why he saw himself justified in publishing *Papalagi*. He says he betrayed Tuiavii because the world to which he returned was ravaged and disillusioned by the First World War and in dire need of innocence and openness. "We Europeans are once again skeptical about ourselves. We question things for their true meaning and we doubt whether our culture is capable of fulfilling the idealism which lives in all of us. That's why we should not think of ourselves as too learned to let our spirit take in the simple ways of thinking and seeing of this South Sea islander, who is not burdened by any education, whose emotions and observations are still original, and who has the ability to make us see how we deprive ourselves of spirituality and replace it with lifeless idols."

Are these the words of someone who made it all up? I will let the readers judge for themselves. My own excursion into Scheurmann's past ended when I realized that even if I went all the way to Samoa to search for the truth, nothing could entirely clarify the mystery. Even if I were to find that no one by the name of Tuiavii ever existed on the island of Upolu, what would that prove? All it might mean is that Scheurmann indeed talked to a Chief and subsequently changed his name. Or, as Alison Devine Nordström said to me on the telephone recently: "Perhaps it wasn't one chief, but several chiefs, Scheurmann talked to; perhaps it wasn't even a chief, but a regular Samoan." In the end it doesn't really matter from whom it is that Scheurmann has taken the wisdom contained in the *Papalagi*, which is where the intellectual search for truth comes to an end.

At that stage, only the spiritual core of Tuiavii's words is left to see, and in it truth shines bright as a beacon. Whether the words printed in the *Papalagi* are indeed those of Chief Tuiavii, or whether they encompass what Scheurmann found in Samoa and himself put into words, they are words of wisdom. And, insofar as all great art contains the essence of truth and affects people deeply, Tuiavii's speeches are great art. After one more World War, five decades of unbridled materialism and the ravaging of much of the world's resources, they ring even more true and relevant than they must have in 1920. Many of the fears expressed by Tuiavii have become reality; for one, the way of life of Samoa's islanders and that of countless other cultures have been drawn into what Tuiavii saw as an orbit of darkness. His recognition that ours is a culture that is economically successful, but spiritually bereft, may have drawn amused chuckles at the beginning of this century, but is widely seen as accurate as it draws to an end. In fact, the imbalance between our material needs and our spiritual well-being is probably the central challenge to our time.

EPILOGUE

Given the evolution of modern Western society, many of Tuiavii's recommendations for change are impractical and unrealizable. But this is not to say that his perspective is not as refreshing, innocent and valid today as it was during his lifetime. No matter which of his comments we think about, we are a bit closer to the truth than we were the moment before. Tuiavii's words give us the most valuable gift imaginable—a mirror in which to see ourselves.

Peter C. Cavelti

I don't tell you the facts; I tell you the truth.

Stephanie Rayner, Canadian artist

He said true things, but called them by wrong names.

Robert Browning

We all know that art is not truth. Art is a lie that makes us realize the truth.

Pablo Picasso

ABOUT PETER C. CAVELTI

Peter C. Cavelti, who translated Tuiavii's speeches and wrote the Introduction and Epilogue to this edition, was born in Switzerland and now lives in Canada. He is the author of several books and numerous essays and articles which have been published internationally.